LET'S BE THE WOMEN

and let the men be the men

By Pastor Frannie Scaglione

Let's Be the Women and Let the Men Be the Men
ISBN: 979-8-9903556-0-6
Copyright © 2024 by Life Transforming Ministries
6500 Winegard Rd
Orlando, FL 32809

1st edition 2024

Dedication

I dedicate this book to my pastors, the late Pastor Greg Powe and Pastor Deborah Powe. Thank you for your mentorship and always being godly examples. We wouldn't have a vision or Life Transforming Ministries if it weren't for you. We love and appreciate you.

Thank you to my children, Asha, Ariel, Nick IV, and my grandchildren for your support and encouraging words. You all are the best!

I want to give special thanks to my daughter, Athena. Thank you for keeping me focused and on track. I couldn't have done it without you. I love you!

To my beloved Nick, we have journeyed through many different seasons of life. Thank you for all the great adventures we've had together and the challenges we've overcome. It made us the people we are today. If I had to do it all over again, I would. You are my BFF and truly my hero! I love you with all my heart.

Table of Contents

Preface

Could your marriage use a little boost or a total renovation? Do you need practical advice to strengthen your relationship? Then I want to encourage you to read my book, *Let's Be the Women, and Let the Men Be the Men.*

I'm Pastor Frannie, Senior Pastor of Life Transforming Ministries. I have been married for forty years, and I understand that a thriving marriage is all about teamwork and alignment. My book is about discovering and unlocking your SUPERPOWER as a woman. As a woman, you have the power to empower! You may have just been using it in the wrong way.

I believe God has given me the roadmap to having a successful marriage. For years, I couldn't understand the ins and outs of marriage: why it was difficult to communicate with one another, why I needed to submit, why I didn't feel heard and valued, and why things seemed so unfair for women in marriage. I would like to share the roadmap for a successful marriage with you through my book!

So why wait? Take advantage of the opportunity to fortify your connection, strengthen your marriage, and love being married! LET'S BE THE WOMEN and let the men be the men will take you through necessary step towards cultivating a fulfilling and thriving marriage.

Introduction

Writing this book was a labor of love and I'm excited to share parts of my story with you. With chapters on "Did God Make Us Equal?", "Why Marriage is Hard", and "How To Empower Your Man and Get Your Needs Met," this book is based entirely on the Word of God and is a must-read for any woman looking to build a strong, happy, and lasting marriage. Now, any woman can glean something from this book. However, this book is intended for married couples, not couples who are dating, as the dynamics and issues are very different for singles. For couples cohabitating, continue to walk toward God and apply these principles you read about in this book, and I believe it will lead you to marriage.

I want to give you a glimpse into my past so you can hear my heart as you read this book. This book chronicles a small portion of Pastor Nick and my life together. As you read, it is essential for you not only to see my results, but also to understand the years of trial and error, guided by the principles of God, that I have followed to have the marriage you see today.

I grew up in the Baptist church, receiving baptism at age five, and I strongly believed in God. I observed many marriages, including those of my parents, my older sister, and couples at church, which allowed me to see the highs and lows of marriage.

My parents were born in the 1920s in Alabama and married in their teens. They had ten children and I was the youngest. My father was a prominent community member, a World War II veteran, a business owner, and a pastor. My dad was a great father.

He was a provider and a protector, and my mom was a loyal and great caregiver. But, like most couples of their era, they struggled to love each other as God intended. It wasn't until my father was near death that he genuinely appreciated the love and loyalty his wife, my mother, gave him for over fifty years.

Although my parents had a strong marriage foundation, I realized early on that marriage was difficult. You would think that would have deterred me from marriage, but I believed marriage was from God. In addition, my parents taught me that shacking up and having sex outside the marriage covenant was a sin, and I didn't want to live in sin — so I chose marriage.

When I started dating Nick, he swept me off my feet! I married him, believing that no one could love and treat me as well as he did. I didn't have Hollywood's ideal of the perfect marriage, however, I believed marrying Nick honored God's plan for my life and we would survive as a couple. We had our first child soon after Nick and I were married at 19.

We planned for me to return to work, but after seeing our child, I realized she might have difficulty being biracial, and I felt staying at home was the best option. Forty years ago, interracial marriages were frowned upon and rare.

So, Nick started a business named National Automotive Marketing Services (NAMS), which became quite profitable for our family. This business was a huge undertaking, almost like working two full-time jobs, so I did my best to support my husband. In addition to raising our children and maintaining a household, I cooked for his employees, prepared car maintenance packets, and washed and ironed their work shirts.

Despite the financial success of the business, we still struggled financially. We have all faced financial struggles, but ours were due to poor money management rather than a lack of money, which was upsetting. At this point in my marriage, I realized Nick struggled with a gambling addiction. At times, Nick gambled money faster than he could make it, and our family suffered due to his addiction. There were constant calls from creditors due to unpaid bills, car repossessions, and the occasional utility disconnection.

During the beginning years of our marriage, Nick would often stay out all night, usually returning home the following morning, but sometimes not coming home for days. I was sure he had a mistress.

On two occasions, I worked up the nerve to follow and confront him. I loaded our now three children into the car and tracked him down. When I got there with my kids and my .38 handgun in the car, I saw Nick sitting at a gambling table all night and not a woman in sight.

Nick's gambling addiction blighted our marriage for over a decade. I remember on our 10th Anniversary, we took a trip to Las Vegas to celebrate. I decided to go to the casino with Nick and didn't think he would gamble away all of our vacation money, however, that's exactly what happened. Then when we came across a pawn shop on the Vegas strip, Nick demanded that I give him all my gold jewelry, including my wedding ring, so that he could continue gambling. I was shocked, angry and hurt, Nick quickly took the money back to casino, and I was left wandering the Vegas Strip alone, questioning my marriage.

Despite all of this, we also had good times. One thing about Nick, he is resourceful and a go-getter. He always found a way to provide what we needed. One Christmas, we didn't have money for a Christmas tree for the girls and Nick knew how important this was to me.
So, he had the brilliant idea to trade his business' car maintenance program for a Christmas tree. I was so happy he made that happen for us. Nick always ensured we had food in our house and a roof over our heads.

He also allowed me to stay home with our children, which was important to me. Whenever a new credit card came in the mail, or he made a big score from gambling, he packed up our family and we headed to Walt Disney World for a week. Nick loved his family, which made it hard for me to walk away, despite his shortcomings.

When Nick and I were dating, he used to attend my parents' church. My parents were actually the founders of the church, and me and my nine siblings grew up in this church together. When we were dating, Nick would always follow me to church.
During that time, I remember Deacon Lawson, who worked for IBM, was a member of my father's church and served him with the utmost faithfulness and respect. Nick was particularly impressed by how Deacon Lawson, an educated man, could serve and submit to my father, a farmer with only a 2nd-grade education.

However, after Nick and I married, he stopped attending church. Despite this, I continued to pray for Nick's return to church, and finally, after fifteen years, he did! I was skeptical but happy with his decision.

At that point, my father had passed away, and Deacon Lawson had become Pastor Lawson. Nick preferred to attend Pastor Lawson's church instead of my family's church because he remembered Pastor Lawson's genuine servanthood towards my father.

My family was outraged about Nick's decision to take me away from the church I had grown up in all my life, but I supported my husband's choice. The Bible teaches that married couples should "leave and cleave to each other, forsaking all others," so I followed Nick.

Despite Pastor Lawson's church being an hour commute each way, Nick and I decided to join St. Mary Missionary Baptist Church in Parrish, FL. We were members there for several years. During that time, Nick began following Pastor Creflo A. Dollar on Christian television. After listening to Pastor Dollar, Nick realized that the Word of God had more to offer than what the traditional Baptist church taught. One of the issues for Nick was seeing the body of Christ scrape by and struggle their whole lives. Pastor Dollar was teaching Biblical prosperity, something we had never heard before. Nick knew there should be more to his walk with Christ, and he knew Pastor Dollar's church was where we needed to be, so he said, "Let's move to Georgia."

We went to Georgia looking for a house and a location to open up a restaurant. After an entire week, nothing worked out. We couldn't find a house or a decent location for a restaurant. Honestly, I felt overwhelmed but kept my concerns to myself because Nick was seeking God, stepping out on big faith, and still trying to find his way.

We eventually chose to return to Tampa. However, before making our way back, we discovered that Pastor Dollar was hosting the International Covenant Ministries (ICM) conference at World Changers Church the same week we were there, so we decided to attend. After the conference, we grabbed something to eat at Mrs. Winners Chicken, and while there, Nick saw someone who attended the ICM meeting wearing a lapel pin with "RTM" written on it. Curious about the pin, Nick asked and she explained that RTM, Revealing Truth Ministries is a church in Tampa, Florida, led by Pastor Powe, who happens to be Pastor Dollar's son.

Nick was so excited to learn that Pastor Dollar had a spiritual son in Tampa. We immediately left Georgia and returned to Tampa, and as soon as we got back, Nick dropped us off at home and went to find Pastor Powe's church. When Nick arrived, he went into RTM's Faith Food store. Coming out of the store, he saw a man walking towards him in the parking lot. It was Pastor Powe. Nick shared with him that he had just returned from Georgia, and that God had told him to start a ministry. Nick and I attended service at Revealing Truth Ministries (RTM) that following Wednesday evening; we knew we were in the right place and became members that very night.

After joining, we began serving at Revealing Truth Ministries. Nick was always an outgoing person, so naturally, he would speak to Pastor Powe and the leaders at the church with ease. Meanwhile, I was still very shy, avoiding lengthy conversations, but I would always smile and give a quick "hi" and "bye" to Pastor

Powe or Pastor Deborah. Nick bragged to Pastor Powe's son about how he made the best lasagna, which got back to Pastor Powe. So he ended up making lasagna and salad for Pastor Powe and his family, and he asked me to make a peach cobbler to go along with it. After the Powe family had eaten the meal, they said, "Man, who made that PEACH COBBLER?!" When Nick told them it was me, that started the routine of me cooking for them a few times a month, which made me nervous. But I was honored to serve the man of God and his family in this capacity because I believe this assignment was orchestrated by God. Whenever Nick delivered the food to Pastor Powe's home, he would invite him in. Pastor Powe would share the Word of God with Nick for hours, which forged a great father-and-son relationship.

Nick submitted to Pastor Powe and did everything Pastor Powe told him to do, even regarding our finances. With his business NAMS, Nick was making six figures but mismanaging the finances; I never knew what was coming in or going out. Pastor Powe told Nick he needed to be accountable and transparent about our finances. Pastor Powe advised him to close NAMS, our business and take a job with a steady paycheck. Closing NAMS was a big deal because it was a considerable pay cut. Although it was tough, Nick obeyed Pastor Powe's instructions.

Throughout our time at RTM, Pastor Powe always stressed the importance of family to Nick. When Nick asked how he could serve him better, Pastor Powe said, "Focus on your family because they are essential to where God is taking you." We planned on staying at RTM for two years before starting our own ministry. However, God had us at RTM for almost thirteen years before Pastor Powe released us to start our ministry.

While at RTM, we made a complete 360-degree pivot in our lives. For the first time, we had our finances in order; we had money saved, we purchased two homes and an IRS tax lien of over $200k was miraculously released, all while taking a massive pay cut. Nick was also rapidly promoted to management at his job with only a high school education. Additionally, we walked through several health scares and family issues. As Nick obeyed God and our pastors, our lives got into order. I allowed the Word of God and counsel from our pastors to heal the decades of a broken marriage and trust issues I had endured.

When the time was nearing for us to be released to begin our church, I had reservations about the assignment we were embarking upon. I had grown up in church, and Nick was everything the church wasn't. I loved Nick and knew I would follow him to the ends of the Earth, but honestly, I didn't know if he was ready to be a pastor and run a ministry. Being a deacon was good enough - but a pastor?

Nick planned to be at RTM for two years, and here we were, thirteen years in, and he was tired of waiting on Pastor Powe's approval to start the ministry. Nick began to talk about us leaving and starting our own church. I told Nick I wasn't going without the blessing and confirmation that we were ready for our assignment. I knew the work it took to run a ministry, and God would hold us responsible for His people. That was the first time I bucked against Nick's leadership in our forty years of marriage.

We continued faithfully serving at RTM and remained committed to our pastors. Two months later, we received the blessing of Pastor Powe, and then I felt confident that we were ready for our assignment to start the ministry. Nick's most essential lesson during our time at RTM was that ministry is about serving people, not just the functions and duties of the church.

When I look back on our trip to Georgia, I realize it was a family adventure that I will always cherish. We had to walk by faith to get to Revealing Truth Ministries (RTM), the brook God called us to.

At this specific brook, we received the training and development we needed that equipped us to win in life and to move forward to start our own ministry. 1 Kings 17:4-6 says you shall drink from the brook, and I have commanded the ravens to sustain you there [with food]." So he went and did in accordance with the word of the LORD; he went and lived by the brook Cherith, which is east of the Jordan. And the ravens brought him bread and meat in the morning, and bread and meat in the evening; and he would drink from the brook. (1 Kings 17:4-6 AMP)

In 2008, we came to Orlando to start our ministry, Life Transforming Ministries (LTM). We began in an apartment complex meeting center, eventually we moved to rent a space in another church. In 2012, we moved into what is now the first LTM Life Center, and in June of 2021, we completely paid off the building. In the years since we began our ministry, Nick has moved up to C-level executive positions in several companies. He earned his first million dollars, and he and I are closer than ever!

Do we still have disagreements? Absolutely! We are human, but we have shared our testimony, counseled others, and watched their lives change the same way our lives have changed. I would love to say there is a 12-step process to a successful marriage, but that would be disingenuous. Even after forty years of marriage, we still seek God and learn new and better ways to love each other. My intention with this book is to encourage you that God can transform your relationship no matter where you are in your marriage. You can embark on a transformative journey if you're willing to trust and believe in God, obey His teachings, and engage in honest self-reflection.

With love, Pastor Frannie

Chapter 1

Did God Make Us Equal?

The big discussion today is whether men and women are equal.

Before we get into the topic of equality, I want to speak to the women. I intend to dispel and undo years of lousy doctrine; God's design for marriage has been twisted and warped for years. Some of the terms and phrases used by God in His word have been modified. For example, the Bible tells women to have a meek and quiet spirit. Well, if I say the word "meek," most of us picture a woman who's a doormat. Everyone walks over her because she won't speak up for herself. However, being meek means she is patient, restrained, and not easily provoked! The power that comes from a meek and quiet spirit shows wisdom and control over your emotions and the situation. So, being meek is a great thing!

God designed all Christians, including men, not just women, to submit. Ephesians 5:21 AMPC says: "Be subject to one another out of reverence for Christ (the Messiah, the Anointed One)." However, the only time submission is brought up is when discussing wives submitting to their husbands. Both men and women are required to submit to each other, but in different ways, as a service to the Lord.

Submission is for everyone. I want to show you how to submit the way God intended. More importantly, I want to demonstrate how submission in marriage is not just the duty of the woman, but the duty of the woman and the man. I want to show women how submission to their husbands can draw their husbands not only to them but to Christ.

Hear me clearly, I am NOT saying that if you are in an abusive situation, you should be waiting for God to change your husband. If you are being physically abused, get out now! Yes, God can change your husband. No, your husband may not allow God to change him. Regardless of what God can do, God is NOT calling you to be hurt while waiting on Him. That is NOT Biblical, God loves you. God does not give a spouse the right to abuse one of HIS children. Submission is not a way to get your spouse to stop abusing you, nor does submission somehow give your spouse permission to abuse you. Abuse is wrong. Never stay in an abusive relationship. Get to safety. Find a Christian counselor. Work on healing, boundaries, and restoration from a safe distance.

Gender Roles

A big idea I want to unpack is understanding godly gender roles. Religion has perpetuated the belief that men are entitled to women's submission and honor, and society reinforces this ideal. The idea of gender roles is a very black-and-white concept, right? It's the assignment: the woman does the dishes, the man does the work, etc. The Bible does not say that the only thing a woman can do is clean the house and raise the children. In the world's version of marriage, gender roles are assignments. In God's design, marital roles are based on what is best for the team!

When God created Adam, He realized that man needed a helper to stand beside him. So, God created Eve from Adam's flesh; this is why we still talk about men and women becoming one when they marry. Genesis 2:21-23 says, And the Lord God caused a deep sleep to fall upon Adam, and he slept: and he took one of his ribs, and closed up the flesh instead thereof; And the rib, which the Lord God had taken from man, made him a woman, and brought her unto the man. And Adam said: This is now bone of my bones And flesh of my flesh; She shall be called Woman, Because she was taken out of Man. (Genesis 2:21-23 KJV)

Men and women are different but are not superior to each other. Instead, we are designed as unique creations of God to complement one another. Spiritually, men and women are equally valuable.

We know that we're different physically — that's obvious! Our physical bodies are different, but despite that, God sees both sexes as valuable. We know that through the Holy Trinity, God said, "Let us make man in our image." The Holy Trinity is God the Father, God the Son, and God the Holy Spirit. They are all one God, with three different roles, as illustrated in Genesis 1:26 where God says, "Let Us [Father, Son, and Holy Spirit] make mankind in Our image, after Our likeness, and let them have complete

19

authority over the fish of the sea, the birds of the air, the [tame] beasts, and over all of the earth, and over everything that creeps upon the earth." (Genesis 1:26 AMPC)

Men and women are created in the image and likeness of God, each with their distinct roles. Think about it: what you do at church differs from what you do at home or in the marketplace. Men and women can do multiple things and be the same person. There is no contradiction in that. Why? Because God also plays multiple roles, and we are created in His image and likeness. In what other ways did God stress that both men and women hold equal value in His sight? Genesis 1:28 says, "Then God blessed them, and God said to them, 'Be fruitful and multiply; fill the earth and subdue it; have dominion over the fish of the sea, over the birds of the air, and over every living thing that moves on the earth." (Genesis 1:26 AMPC)

When God talks about 'them' in this context, he's talking about both men and women, He's referring to humanity. He is saying to us, both men and women, "You have dominion, power, and authority. I have given this to you." We (men and women) have dominion over all the fish, all the fowl, and over all the Earth. The book of Genesis shows us that God created humans to be equal; men are not superior to women, and men are not presumed to be the only leaders. We see from scripture that men and women are equal to each other, and both have dominion over the earth. The Old Testament clearly shows that women lend men their strength to be fruitful together. Nothing in the book of Genesis' account of creation, BEFORE THE FALL OF MANKIND, says that men have higher status or authority over women — they are one. As the story goes, together, they give in to temptation. Genesis 3:6 says, "And when the woman saw that the tree was good for food and that it was pleasant to the eyes, and a tree to be desired to make one wise, she took off the fruit thereof, and did eat, and gave also unto her husband with her; and he did eat." (Genesis 3:6 KJV)

God then speaks directly to both of them to share the specific consequences of their sin. Men's hierarchy over women is not in God's original design. So, it makes sense to say that if man's superiority over a woman resulted from the fall, then man couldn't have ruled over us before the fall. We should not buy into the mistaken idea that women should not use the authority that God gave them.

Let's walk through the scriptures and look at many women of the Bible and their positions in the marketplace, in government, and in the church. You will quickly see that God not only intended for women to be equal, but in many cases, women were the leaders.

Women in the Old Testament

The Old Testament describes women, including wives and mothers, in leadership roles with God's blessing. Women in the Bible ruled over nations, armies, and businesses:

- Miriam is best known for leading the Hebrew women in song and dance after crossing the Red Sea and for her role in helping deliver Moses from the Nile River (Exodus 15:20-21 AMPC); (Exodus 2 KJV).

- Deborah saves Israel from its enemies. She is the leader of Israel, a wife, and a mother who has the authority to command the most experienced military commanders (Judges 4:6 -14 KJV).

- Queen Esther influenced the destruction of the House of Haman (Esther 7:1–10 KJV).

- Huldah, a prophetess, has the king, elders, prophets, and people accepting her Word as revelation from God, Himself. (2 Chronicles 34:22–32 KJV).

The Old Testament clearly states that women in religious and political leadership roles were typical and expected. Women have been promoted by God to prophetic roles and are seen speaking key portions of inspired Scripture, such as the Songs of Miriam,

Hannah's prayer, the Songs of Elizabeth, and the Songs of Mary
(the Magnificat).

And Miriam answered them:
"Sing to the Lord,
For He has triumphed gloriously!
The horse and its rider
He has thrown into the sea!" (Exodus 15:21 NKJV).

And Hannah prayed and said:
"My heart rejoices in the Lord;
My horn is exalted in the Lord.
I smile at my enemies,
Because I rejoice in Your salvation.

No one is holy like the Lord,
For there is none besides You,
Nor is there any rock like our God

Talk no more so very proudly;
Let no arrogance come from your mouth,
For the Lord is the God of knowledge;
And by Him actions are weighed.

The bows of the mighty men are broken,
And those who stumbled are girded with strength.

Those who were full have hired themselves out for bread,

And the hungry have ceased to hunger.

Even the barren has borne seven,

And she who has many children has become feeble"

(1 Samuel 2:1-5 NKJV).

And Mary prophetically said:

"My soul magnifies the Lord,

And my spirit has rejoiced in God my Savior.

For He has regarded the lowly state of His maidservant;

For behold, henceforth all generations will call me blessed.

For He who is mighty has done great things for me,

And holy is His name." (Luke 1:46–49 NKJV).

It says in the Old Testament that God appointed women to leadership in the church and in the marketplace, so why do we insist on believing otherwise?

Women in the New Testament

Jesus boldly challenged societal norms by valuing and respecting women as equals. He respected women's intelligence and spiritual capacity and was happy to teach them. He shares His wisdom with the Samaritan woman and with Martha during a time when the culture did not believe in educating women. The fact that Jesus encouraged women to be His disciples is not only shocking, but also proof of His agreement that women are equal to men in every way.

What's great about the Samaritan woman is that it shows Jesus truly loves everyone, so much so that He empowered a woman of loose morals to spread the Gospel to other Samaritans. In John 4:10-29 (KJV), Jesus meets this Samaritan woman at Jacob's Well after a morning's journey and disregards social custom by asking her for a drink. This boundary crossing between a Jew and a Samaritan sparks a conversation about their differences. She has a good grasp of her own tradition's and beliefs, so she asks, "Are you greater than our father Jacob who gave us this well?" And yet, she is eager for the eternal abundance Jesus promises.

Jesus promises living water that gives eternal life and invites her to bring the rest of her household—specifically, her husband—to receive the goodness He is offering. This turns the conversation to her personal history and current marital situation. She responds honestly and succinctly, "I have no husband". Jesus affirms that what she has said is true and indicates that she has had five husbands, and she is not married to the man she is living with now; Jesus knew her more thoroughly than she might have guessed.

She immediately understands that He is a prophet who knows and speaks the truth. She decides to take their discussion a step further and asks Him about the proper place for worship, one of the major differences between Jews and Samaritans. In response, Jesus speaks of a future time when all true worshipers of God will worship, not in a particular place, but "in the Spirit and in truth".

25

Jesus' mention of the future raises her hopes for the coming Messiah. She speaks of her anticipation of the fuller understanding she will receive when the Messiah comes. In response, Jesus declares, "I am He."

In a sudden turn, this woman, whom Jesus earlier asked for a drink, has now found her own thirst for understanding quenched. She has met the Messiah, the one she has been hoping for. At that moment, the disciples interrupt their conversation, but she has heard all she needs to hear.
She drops her water jug and rushes back to the village and says to everyone she meets, "Come and see a man who told me everything I have ever done. He cannot be the Messiah, can He?"

The Samaritan woman listens with open attentiveness to Jesus as she asks Him questions about her faith and hope. The longer she talks with Him, the more her understanding grows until she sees the full truth: Jesus is the Messiah. Throughout this conversation, she demonstrates a posture of discipleship, learning from Jesus, and now she is called an evangelist.

The identity of this woman was never revealed, but she was considered the most disadvantaged in society. A female in a society where women were demeaned and disregarded. A woman of the Samaritan race traditionally despised by the Jews, and living in shame as a social outcast. When the woman believed, she immediately ran off to tell the others. Her words made an impact;

many of the Samaritans from her town knew Jesus was the Messiah because of this woman's testimony.

You are fit for any task, just like the women in the Old and New Testaments! Men and women are equal; we both serve God, but just in different ways.

Chapter 2

Women Are Kings in the Marketplace

My goal is to help women really understand the difference between being a godly woman in her marriage and being a KING in the marketplace.

A king? Yes, not a queen: a King!

What characteristics do you think of when you imagine a king? A king has a reputation of wisdom, character, and authority, which applies just as much to women as to men. Of course, there are women with wisdom! We must debunk the myth that women weren't created to be successful outside the home.

In the marketplace, a woman's role is to be a king; her role is the same as a man's. Women are equally responsible for ruling and dominating, just like any other king. Regardless of who she is surrounded by, whether men or women, a godly woman is accountable for reigning as God has called her to do. (Philippians 4:13 NIV) says, "I can do all this through Him who gives me strength."

Let me make it simple. Kings rule! Kings conquer! Kings establish order! Kings have a business mindset.

Women are advancing and doing great things in the marketplace. I know many women, including single moms and married women, with a kingdom mindset. I know these women will take the marketplace by storm because they are God-centered people going after it in the marketplace for the RIGHT reasons. The Bible gives many examples of women working successfully outside the home. Romans 16:1-2 says, "Now I introduce and commend to you our sister Phoebe, a deaconess (servant) of the church at Cenchrea, that you may receive her in the Lord [with love and hospitality], as God's people ought to receive one another. And that you may help her in whatever manner she may require assistance from you, for she has been a benefactor of many, including myself." (Romans 16:1-2 AMP)

Acts 16:14 says, "A woman named Lydia, from the city of Thyatira, a dealer in purple fabrics who was [already] a worshiper of God, listened to us; and the Lord opened her heart to pay attention and to respond to the things said by Paul." (Acts 16:14 AMP)

Some women worked alongside their husbands in their trade. Acts 18:1-3 says,"After this Paul left Athens and went to Corinth. There he met a Jew named Aquila, a native of Pontus, who had recently come from Italy with his wife, Priscilla, because [the Roman Emperor] Claudius had issued an edict that all the Jews were to leave Rome. Paul went to see them, and because he was of the same trade, he stayed with them; and they worked together because they were tent-makers." (Acts 18:1-3 AMP)

God doesn't see our gender; He sees our service. Our gender only plays a part in our marriage. When you are God-centered, you are empowered and given the ability by the Lord to go out and gather wealth to pour it back into His Kingdom. God wants us to prosper to bless others and give them a chance to transform, just as He has blessed and transformed us.

Why is Purpose Important?

Many women are ambitious and have a burning desire to be fulfilled beyond the role of a wife and mother.

It's important to understand that God put this ambition inside you, from the foundation of the world and before your momma knew your daddy. Jeremiah 1:5 says, "Before I formed you in the womb I knew you; Before you were born I sanctified you; I ordained you a prophet to the nations." (Jeremiah 1:5 NKJV)

God wants to use everyone to build His Kingdom. Ephesians 2:10 says, "For we are God's [own] handiwork (His workmanship), recreated in Christ Jesus, [born anew] that we may do those good works which God predestined (planned beforehand) for us [taking paths which He prepared ahead of time], that we should walk in them [living the good life which He prearranged and made ready for us to live]." (Ephesians 2:10 AMPC)

God is about productivity and increase, and He has given everyone talents, abilities and qualities to bless others. Many people don't realize that giving, and not getting, is the way for you to walk in true prosperity. Luke 6:38 says, "Give, and you will receive. Your gift will return to you in full—pressed down, shaken together to make room for more, running over, and poured into your lap. The amount you give will determine the amount you get back." (Luke 6:38 NLT)

People are frustrated because they are looking for careers that will pay them the most money and give them the best status or, they attempt to avoid work and responsibility by lying on the beach all day. In either case, they wonder why their lives aren't fulfilled. They are unfulfilled because they are not in pursuit of discovering their God-given purpose.

Purpose is discovered by pursuing God, taking risks, and being courageous. When we excessively worry about what others think, have an imbalanced need to please people, or chase after money and pleasure, it will take us off the path of discovering our purpose. Purpose is not found; it's not a brand, an "aha" moment, or a big event. Godly purpose is discovered while you are on the journey of pursuing God. Your purpose is the reason behind why you do what you do. It is what inspires you and what you truly value. God chooses your purpose and you discover it! When God decided your purpose, He graced you with the endowment to do it. You will become happy and undisturbed once you discover your purpose. This gift will make room for you, it will be fulfilling, sweatless, and bring prosperity to you. Through your purpose, God could give you a level of anointing that possibly no one else has, and you should be excited!

Kings are Motivated by Profits

Can I get an Amen?!

In the old days, women were homemakers and did what they were told, but they also made pies and cakes to sell within their community. Women have always been creative and entrepreneurial; it's part of what God put in them. Although insecure men may try to hold women back, God has placed things on the inside of you that have changed and will continue to CHANGE THE WORLD.

I want to give you a little insight into my journey. This is the story of Sallie B's Pies.

One evening, my girls and I were playing in the yard when our neighbor walked up and said he wanted to eat my dog. This particular neighbor was a known problem on our street, often threatening his own grandmother! So I asked him if he wanted ketchup to go along with it. Nick was not at home and I didn't want him to think I was afraid. Knowing Nick, he was probably out gambling with his friends. Later that night, I heard something outside and I thought about the neighbor we were having issues with earlier. I called Nick and asked him to come home because I was afraid. He replied that we were fine and the guy was most likely all talk, and if I needed the gun, it was in the closet.

His response broke my heart. I was home alone with three children under the age of seven, and he couldn't come five minutes up the road to make sure we were safe? Angrily, I packed up my children, grabbed my .38 handgun and went looking for him. Sure enough, I found him at Fatso's Sports Bar. I walked in abruptly, and Nick looked like he had seen a ghost. Nick got up quickly from the card table and rushed me outside. I guess he feared what I might say or do in front of his gambling buddies. I yelled in his face that our marriage was over and a few other choice words! I got in my car, slammed the door, and sped out of the parking lot.

I thought Nick would come after me to apologize and convince me to stay in our marriage. Instead, he came home the following afternoon. For the first time in almost ten years, I knew when Nick didn't come after me, that I was done with our marriage. That morning I called my dad; I told him I needed a job. My dad knew I had no interest in working outside the home, and my priority was my children. My dad told me I could be the baker for our family's restaurant. I didn't have a reliable car at the time,so gave me a truck to deliver pies and money to buy products to start baking. So I went out, got my supplies, went home, and got to work.

Later, Nick came home, saw my dad's truck in the driveway, and thought my dad was there. Instead, he walked into boxes of yams and dough spread across the kitchen. He had tons of questions, "What are you doing? Why is this stuff here? What is this?"

I told him, "If you must know, I'm now the new bakerrrr for the BBQ pit." I rolled my eyes and kept baking. He was quietly shocked that I had secured a job and was standing on what I told him the night before. He realized that my threat to leave was more than an empty one. I never made threats I didn't intend to stand on, so this was the first time he'd heard that from me in almost ten years

Now I must admit, the first batch of pies was a complete disaster; customers were returning them, and my family laughed and joked about my failure. I also laughed with them, but I felt a little hurt inside. It was the first venture I had ever tried, so it was tough to fail and be mocked by my own family. However, I did not allow that to deter me because I had no other skills, and it was all I had. I was determined to make it work.

I went to see my mom, Tampa's best Sweet Potato Pie maker! We sat in her kitchen for hours, perfecting the recipe. Like most homemakers of her era, my mom didn't keep recipes or measure anything; she cooked and baked by sight and feel. It wasn't two teaspoons of this, it was a dash, a pinch, or my personal favorite, a "right smarta". She would pour, and I would measure. So with my recipe in hand, I ran home to whip up batch number two! I returned to the restaurant with my second batch, and what do you know, it was a hit!

When I say, "It was a hit," they couldn't keep the pies on the shelves.

Once Nick saw that I was serious his entire attitude changed. He did an about-face. He started being nice to me and wanted to converse with me. He even moved us into a beautiful new house. He respected me in a way I had never seen before. For the first time, I think he realized that I wasn't with him because I needed him; I was with him because I loved him. I had never felt that kind of accomplishment and pride before.

Anything that doesn't evolve and grow will die! It's essential to find time to develop yourself. You may not be able to return to college full-time, but take a class, create a business plan, or take a trade. It is important to make sure that you stay relevant. In those days, it wasn't easy because there weren't any online classes or work-from-home jobs. Remember, there are seasons to life, but you should always look for ways to be an asset to the team and prepare for the next phase of your life. Don't get me wrong, being a stay-at-home mom was some of the best years of my life, playing with my children and watching them grow up. I quickly noticed when I owned my business, Nick was compelled to involve me in decisions and seemed more transparent about things I wouldn't have known. We operated more as a team.

So, now I'm an "independent woman" making my own money! Keep in mind that I did the business as my exit plan, and I made Nick aware of it when I started.

However, after moving into the new home, feeling more accomplished because of the business, and seeing more transparency in our relationship, I decided to stay. There were subtle changes at this point; Nick didn't stay out as much as he had before. Don't get it confused: Nick was still a gambler, and there were still a lot of issues between us. But I knew I had to be all in when I decided to stay.

The money I made was OUR MONEY. Yes, I brought my check home like Nick, and we put our money together even though Nick had a gambling addiction. It doesn't make sense, right? Well, I knew I was doing what I was supposed to do as a godly wife. Remember, Nick had always taken care of me despite his addictions. My mom, however, always told me to keep some money on the side just in case things didn't work out. I knew it wasn't a good idea to be secretive, and it wasn't the right thing to do by God. Besides, I didn't like it when Nick spent money gambling behind my back. Let me be clear and bring balance: if you are in a situation where your spouse has an addiction and does not work and take care of his family, it is time for you to show tough love. Tell your husband he must get help because a man MUST work. Until he does this, you must continue providing and caring for your family. As 1 Timothy 5:8 says, "But if any provide not for his own, and especially for those of his own house, he hath denied the faith, and is worse than an infidel." (1 Timothy 5:8 KJV)

Although I was running a successful business, I also maintained our household by cooking, cleaning, and taking care of our children. The business outgrew my kitchen, I decided to rent a space from my brother in the back of his restaurant. I even made a separate area for my kids to hang out in. My newfound independence and pride in myself helped me take the focus off what Nick wasn't doing. I knew that by doing what was right, I was honoring God.

Sallie B's Pies got so popular that Nick had to help me make deliveries. I was grateful the animosity we had towards each other was slowly disappearing. My husband wasn't intimidated by my success because he knew I was submitted to God and therefore submitted to him and would do what was right. He knew he could trust me. I used the entrepreneurial spirit the Lord gave me, but I didn't change my role as a wife and a mother. My role at my husband's side remained the same because I understood I didn't need to conquer all aspects of my life in every area. Why? Because I was working to be one with my husband. We were becoming a team; it was one cause and one battle. There is no competition in our relationship.

Teamwork Makes the Dreamwork

I see women today who are jealous of their husbands, but jealousy issues often stem from poor self-esteem. The envious person usually does not feel a sense of innate worth. A jealous spouse might harbor unrealistic expectations about marriage. They may have grown up with the fantasy of marriage, thinking married life would be like what they saw in magazines and movies. I want you to know that you no longer need to feel jealous. Walk confidently, knowing that God has graced you with a purpose. Confidence is knowing that you have a purpose. Achieving success is guaranteed when a husband and wife work together as a team and put their trust in God. That trust in God will eradicate fear and eliminate the need to fight for self-preservation. I laugh and tell Nick, "You are blessed because of my obedience to God, and He used you as the vessel." He loves that because he knows he is my hero! God has called women to be their husbands' biggest cheerleaders.

You might ask, how can a strong, independent woman fit into God's vision of an ideal relationship? How can your husband provide and be your protector if you are able to look after yourself?

You need to understand that even if you are the bigger breadwinner, this does not change God's ordained order for marriage and the household. Your husband is still the head of the home.

If you are flaunting your position and salary or weaponizing it against him in the home, it will cause issues in your marriage. Making more money doesn't allow you to step over or bypass your husband in decision-making for the household. It's not your money or his money; it's our money. Many couples are separating their finances, which doesn't foster trust or encourage teamwork. Trust in a marriage isn't just about being physically faithful. Trust is the glue of life. It's the essential ingredient that holds all relationships together and should be in all aspects of marriage. It's about whether you can be trusted with money, whether you are honest about where you are, and whether you keep your word. Trust that we are a team. Trust that you love me for me, not for what you can get from me. Always remember, you reap what you sow. Just because you are up today doesn't mean you won't be completely reliant on him financially in the future. Remember to consider the inevitable seasons of life. You want a husband who will boast about your skills in the marketplace and praise you to his friends and family and not be resentful of you. Leave work at work and make sure you have the right attitude at home, which is a giving, loving, and respectful attitude toward your husband as the head of the house.

A Season for Everything

Every marriage and every relationship has seasons; husbands need to realize there may be a time for him to be elbow-deep in diapers, there is nothing wrong with that. A father teaches discipline and love, he sets an example worth following and prays for his family. Husbands should also know that if his wife financially contributes to the home, there will be times when he has to cook dinner. Household work is not only a woman's job. Remember, this is a team; we are committed to doing whatever it takes for the TEAM to win.

In every team, there will be disagreements. When tough decisions need to be made, and there is no agreement between the two of you, get godly counsel; don't run to your girls. I wouldn't advise discussing marital issues with your friends, especially if they are single. Singles live a different life than married people and often can't relate.

When you decide to share private and intimate details about your marriage with others, you are giving them the information to manipulate the situation, destroy your marriage, or worse, take your husband. Proverbs 6:26 says, "For on account of a prostitute, one is reduced to a piece of bread [to be eaten up], And the immoral woman hunts [with a hook] the precious life [of a man]." A married and committed man that is greatly loved and treasured by his wife and family is considered a precious life! So what is the hook the adulterous woman uses to snare our husbands?" (Proverbs 6:26 AMP)

She seduces him with her sexuality and false flattery, leading him to feel respected and honored. And then you wonder, what does she have that you don't have? Nothing! Oftentimes, when we don't respect and honor our husbands, it leads to them not feeling loved. Consequently, they may become more susceptible to the seduction of other women.

Instead of discussing marital issues with your friends, get wisdom from your pastors or another successful married couple with longevity. If time permits, wait and pray about it. If you are still waiting for agreement, let your husband decide what to do. Empowering him will pay you dividends later because you've shown him honor and respect as the head of the home. It's essential to support your husband's decisions for the team and avoid any actions that may undermine it. Do it the best you can, as long as it doesn't go against the Word of God or cause abuse to you or someone in your family. What happens to a team that doesn't execute well together — they lose the game! Remember, even in marital disagreements, doing tasks you don't love is a service to the Lord, and God will reward you.

Husbands shouldn't be talking to other people about marital problems either. Some men fail to realize women are competitive, just like they are, but in different ways. At first glance, men are more prone to competition than women. They can be more risk-tolerant and use more physical aggression toward each other. Their friendships are, by and large, transactional, and their conflicts are typically straightforward. On the other hand, women often experience emotional depth and complexity in friendship and competition. If women seem less competitive than men, it's because they act covertly and underhanded.

Some women are jealous, competitive, scorned, and give advice from a place of hurt. Especially so in the era we are living in today because you have something they don't have: a husband. Often, women are competitive because they don't feel good enough, which results in competition with others as they try to prove to themselves that they are good enough in some way. Competition also stems from the need to be accepted. After they've won against other women, competitive women may feel they can achieve the approval that they've sought all their lives.

When friends or peers engage in behaviors such as gossiping, negativity, sabotage, gaslighting, nosiness, boasting, mimicking, downplaying your successes, and discrediting you in front of others, they are showing signs of competitive jealousy.

This is why the Bible warns us not to compare ourselves with one another. 2 Corinthians 10:12 says, "We do not have the audacity to put ourselves in the same class or compare ourselves with some who [supply testimonials to] to commend themselves. If they measure themselves by themselves and compare themselves with themselves, they lack wisdom and behave like fools." (2 Corinthians 10:12 AMPC)

Don't compare; you are fearfully and wonderfully made! Psalms 139:14 says, "I praise you because I am fearfully and wonderfully made; your works are wonderful, I know that full well. We are all uniquely, fearfully and wonderfully made." (Psalms 139:14 NIV)

Agreement is vital in marriage. After all, if you can't get along with your boss, you can get another job, and that won't affect your life, but breaking your marriage vows with your husband will have detrimental effects on your life and on your family.

Remember what we talked about before: if you are the boss in the marketplace, then any man working for you needs to be submitted to you. You don't submit to him just because he is a man. If you have a peer that's a man, you don't need to submit to him either; he's not above you; you are his equal. If your peers in the marketplace happen to be men, then you're there to compete with them.

You are there to win if you can! If you're in sales, smash those targets; if you work in a big company, take responsibility for doing your part to improve the team. Whatever your role is, gender should not be a part of the equation. Don't worry about acting ladylike — be Christian-like. This means you are there to reign, rule, and dominate! We have to look to the example of God. He is God the Father, God the Son, and God the Holy Spirit; they are all God, but they serve different functions. You have to remember to change your hat! Wear your King hat in the marketplace and kick butt! You can't be the same person across the board. Your husband isn't just another man; he has a specific place in your life. As I've shown you in the Bible, we are to submit to only ONE MAN in everything: our husbands. Ephesians 5:24 says, "Now as the church submits to Christ, so also wives should submit to their husbands in everything." (Ephesians 5:24 NIV) When you are home, you have to put that King hat away and put on your wife's hat, and God has equipped you with the ability to do so. You don't need a conquering mindset in all areas of your life. You don't need a conquering mindset at home; you are not there to conquer your husband, but to partner with him.

Spiritual growth naturally flows when you obey God. When I chose to submit to my husband rather than demand my own way, God showed favor to me and helped my husband grow. Yes, when a wife submits to her husband, God will grow her husband, even when he isn't seeking God for growth.
Let me clarify …

At this point, my pie business had grown, and I had gotten more contracts. Business was booming, so much so that I became overwhelmed with the growth of it. Nick was working full-time, but that didn't stop him from helping me. To my surprise, Nick didn't try to take over, but did what I asked. He would help with deliveries, baking pies, picking up supplies, and anything else I asked of him. He yielded to my authority! I hear you asking, "Pastor Nick, submitting to his wife? No way!" Yes! It was about the team. Everyone in my family helped, even our children. The girls would watch their brother, cut and package pies, and mix the batter. It was a family effort that flowed smoothly because my leadership in the business didn't threaten the head of the house. It was great, and everybody worked together in that business because it was ours, not mine.

Fast forward a few decades, and the same dynamic still holds true with the church. People in the church submit to me as they submit to my husband. I have Nick's back, and he has mine. Nick holds a full-time job outside Life Transforming Ministries, so I fill in the gaps. When he is out of town working, I preach the sermon. It's never been my job, his job — it's OURS, we work to maintain it and build it. That is the core of marriage: teamwork!

We aren't so focused on creating roles, titles, and assignments; instead, we focus on what needs to be done. Some days you give 100%, and some days you give 50%, but stop keeping score because Satan will remind you of the score every time. You should always give your best in all areas and seek to give the advantage, not to take the advantage.

The way we operate at Life Transforming Ministries, we don't say there are jobs for women, and there are jobs for men. We all do what it takes to get the job done. So, I have shown you, according to scripture, the specific characteristics a woman should possess inside and outside the home. Her children and husband adore her, she is strong and dignified, and she rocks it in the marketplace like the King she is!

Chapter 3

Why is Marriage Hard?

The universal question… "Is it me? Am I the problem?" or "Why doesn't this work for me like it does for other women?"

The most beautiful experiences in life always seem to feature some challenges. We all know that marriage is hard. There's something undeniably profound about two people committing themselves to each other, isn't there? At the same time, there are endless testimonies from married people about the hardships of marital commitment. What exactly is it about marriage that makes it so difficult? What are the most challenging parts of being married?

Believe it or not, it stems from the punishment after the fall of Adam and Eve. In Genesis 3:1-6, we see that one day, Satan came disguised as a snake and spoke to Eve, convincing her to eat the fruit from the tree of good and evil. Eve told the serpent that God said they should not eat it and they would die if they did. But Satan tempted Eve to eat, saying that she would become like God if she did. Eve believed the lie and took a bite of the fruit. She then gave some to Adam for him to eat. (Genesis 3:1-6 NKJV)
Adam and Eve, now knowing that they had sinned, immediately felt ashamed and tried to hide from God. Eve usurped God's authority; she tempted and controlled Adam by giving him something she knew he shouldn't have. God did not blame Eve alone. Adam, who

was with her, stood by silently (passively) while she was tempted, and seeing nothing happen, he joined in. They both shared in disobedience and brought disaster to themselves.

In reading this story, you will notice that nothing happened until both Adam and Eve ate the fruit. That's when they immediately felt and saw the consequences of their sin. This supports the fact that we become one flesh when we marry.

Adam and Eve were not cursed, but punished. They were given permanent reminders of what they had done: Eve's life would be marked by pain in childbearing and strain in the marriage relationship. Genesis 3:16 says, "Unto the woman he said, 'I will greatly multiply thy sorrow and thy conception; in sorrow thou shalt bring forth children; and thy desire shall be to thy husband, and he shall rule over thee." (Genesis 3:16 KJV)

Let's discuss the meaning of the word "desire" in this scripture. It refers to the craving for our husbands to validate us emotionally. We need them to be pleased with us because we care about what they think, which then gives them control over us because we desire their validation.

In punishment for Adam's passivity, God made him the head of the marriage. As punishment for Eve's controlling spirit, God made her submit to her husband, resulting in marriage being hard. Man's greatest fear is to be the leader of his family, and he will be held responsible and accountable to God for the success or failure of his marriage. As part of his punishment, Adam must work hard for their food until he dies. Genesis 3:17 says, "To Adam he said, Because you listened to your wife and ate fruit from the tree about which I commanded you, 'You must not eat from it," 'Cursed is the ground because of you; through painful toil you will eat food from it all the days of your life. It will produce thorns and thistles for you, and you will eat the plants of the field. By the sweat of your brow you will eat your food until you return to the ground, since from it you were taken; for dust you are and to dust you will return." (Genesis 3:17 NIV)

In looking at Eve, we now understand why women sometimes struggle with feelings of not being enough. This feeling has nothing to do with us, but stems from Eve's punishment in the garden, which resulted in the need for validation.

When some women feel invalidated, it can lead to an increased desire for control. However, there are many reasons why wives may attempt to control their husbands. They may feel afraid of losing control over their own lives and take on the spirit of Eve. These reasons may stem from their past experiences, their upbringing, their husband's lack of emotional support, or not trusting their husbands' ability to lead. In reality, both parties are fearful in their marital roles. The husband is afraid to lead, and the wife is afraid to submit. A resentful wife may say she is just strong-willed; she doesn't need her husband, or no man will tell her what to do. "I can think for myself!" that's the ranting of a woman scorned. Hell has no fury like a woman scorned! I like to say it this way: "Hell has no fury, like a woman's emotions that are not validated."

Validation is an essential part of human interaction. It's a critical communication tool for expressing acceptance and connection within relationships. Safe and secure relationships make space for each person to feel their emotions are respected. Emotional invalidation is when those emotions are not respected, and the other person views your feelings as irrational, unreasonable, or makes you feel like you don't have good ideas and qualities. When emotions are not validated, it makes people feel as though their emotional experience is wrong. They may think that their emotions are unacceptable, insignificant, or inaccurate. This invalidation is the worst heartache and pain because it's coming from the person that you love.

Emotional invalidation can lead to considerable confusion and self-doubt. The invalidated person may question their reality or their response to things. This insecurity can lead to self-blame and feelings of low self-worth. Invalidation can be one of the most damaging issues in a relationship.

There is a story of a man who died and went to heaven to find two signs above two lines. One sign said: "ALL THOSE MEN WHO HAVE BEEN DOMINATED BY THEIR WIVES, STAND HERE." That line of men seemed to stretch off through the clouds into infinity.

The second sign read: "ALL THOSE WHO HAVE NEVER BEEN DOMINATED BY THEIR WIVES, STAND HERE." Underneath the sign stood one man.

The man who had just arrived in heaven approached the single man, grabbed his arm, and said, "What's the secret? How did you do it? That other line has millions of men, and you are the only one standing in this line." The man looked around, puzzled, and said, "Why, I am not sure I know. My wife just told me to stand here." We have all heard jokes about "who wears the pants in the family." Yet leadership in the home is no laughing matter.

Another reason marriage is hard is because, during the last few decades, our culture has redefined the meaning and responsibilities of men and women in society and the home. Many men are confused and insecure and do not know how to lead in the home. Growing up, they needed a better model for leadership and had no mental picture of what it meant to lead a family.

The teachings of the New Testament clearly show the biblical ideal of marriage as two people willingly seeking to meet each other's needs. Mutual respect and consideration are the marks of a Christian marriage. Wives, controlling your husbands won't work if you want mutual respect and a wonderful marriage. Similarly, husbands who degrade their wives by neglect or insensitive and abusive treatment won't work either. One cause of the feminist movement may have been that men abandoned God's design. When God presented Eve to Adam in the garden, Adam received her as a gift of great value from God to himself. Proverbs 18:22 says, "When a husband finds a wife, he finds a treasure." (Proverbs 18:22 NLT) When husbands, particularly Christians, do not treat their wives as gifts from God and helpmates, they are not following God's design.

"Head" does not mean male dominance, where a man lords over a woman and demands her total obedience to his every wish and command. God never viewed women as second-class citizens. God's word clearly states that men and women are all equally His creation and are of equal value and worth to Him.

Today we see a great movement toward refraining from marriage from both men and women. Please do not think avoiding marriage will exempt you from life's difficulties. Trying to avoid one pit, you will end up in a deeper pit. Marriage is the training ground for emotional intelligence and winning in life. Obeying God in marriage takes away selfishness and brings personal development needed to overcome obstacles and achieve victory IN EVERY AREA OF YOUR LIFE. Romans 5:3-4 says, "Moreover [let us also be full of joy now!] let us exult and triumph in our troubles and rejoice in our sufferings, knowing that pressure and affliction and hardship produce patient and unswerving endurance. And endurance (fortitude) develops maturity of character (approved faith and tried integrity). And character [of this sort] produces [the habit of] joyful and confident hope of eternal salvation." (Romans 5:3-4 AMPC)

Marriage is also difficult because of misunderstandings of the word submission. Say the word submission if you want to start a heated debate among Christian women. You will likely hear a litany of strong opinions about whether or not it is even relevant in our society today, followed by questioning whether or not it has any practical function in the 50/50 marriage, which should be 100/100 because you can't bring half of yourself to the table of anything you hope to achieve!

Benefits of Submission

True submission is not weakness — it's actually a hidden power. It's not just about pleasing your husband; it's about pleasing the Father through submitting and loving your husband. The power of submission is beautiful when we use it as God intended. However, our power (attitude, behavior, and sexuality) can also be destructive when misused. Think of it this way: The strongest man (Samson), the wisest man (Solomon), and the Godliest man (David) were all compromised by the power of women. In these situations, feminine power was used for harm, instead of good. Are you using your power to build up or to tear down?

As a pastor and a Christian who believes the Bible is the authoritative Word of God, I've seen many single, married, and divorced women struggle with this submission topic. God's design for marriage includes submission, which is one of those biblical teachings that can frustrate and offend Christian women.

Many women reject the idea of a husband as a leader, considering it outdated and impractical for modern times. Despite being written in a particular place and time, we must accept that the Bible is an unchanging truth that calls us to be servants of God in every area of life, including marriage. Hebrews 13:8 says, "Jesus Christ is the same yesterday and today and forever." (Hebrews 13:8 NIV)

I know what you are thinking. How can I submit to a man? Men act like children. They are selfish beings, and those that aren't, are weak and passive. Who wants to be led by a fool or a wimp? Even the leaders (or alpha males as they call themselves), may mistreat or ignore women. Women tend to be responsible, organized, and more mature. We should be the leaders by default! If we don't take the lead, aren't we spitting in the face of what God has bestowed upon us? If God wanted men to lead, why make women so formidable?

Yes, but our power is not exercised through control, like Eve, but through our godly actions, not just our words. Proverbs 14:12 says, "There is a way which seems right to a man and appears straight before him, but at the end of it is the way of death." (Proverbs 14:12 AMPC)

To submit is to take the divinely ordered place in a relationship because that's the role God has called the wife to be in. Submission can never be required by another human being. It can only be given based on trust, to believe God's word, and to be willing to learn and grow in your marriage.

In Eve's punishment, God created a failsafe for our success and fulfillment. He gave wives the need for their husband's approval, which was meant to prevent Satan from exploiting our power. Think about it: Satan easily deceived Eve. And as a result, she brought sin into the whole world. Satan tempted her with the beauty of the apple and the thirst for knowledge. By requiring wives to submit to their husbands and obtain their agreement, God prevented Satan from deceiving us again.

As you submit to God by way of your husband, you will be redeemed from the punishment of Eve. You will be free from the excessive need for approval from your husband, including your children and parents. You won't depend on others for your self-worth anymore because you will know who you are. You will receive one of God's greatest rewards: God's validation. You will experience a sense of self-worth, identity, emotional stability, love, hope, joy, and peace. Proverbs 16:7 says, "When a man's ways please the LORD, he maketh even his enemies be at peace with him." (Proverbs 16:7 KJV)

When God grows us spiritually through being submitted, He matures us emotionally. Our emotional growth can be achieved by accepting that God has more knowledge than we do.

The problem is we think everything should be fair, causing us to take our focus off God's promises and stop believing. The world is utterly selfish, and it will never be fair! When we receive God, He gives us his undeserved favor, which is far better because He is the creator and He owns the whole world. We grow as we see God move through our obedience. It will mature us to be okay with letting God be God. You don't have to try to do God's job. Move out of the way, and you will see God do His job perfectly! Peace comes when you allow God to be God. When you refuse to let your husband lead, you are telling God He doesn't have control. "You see what my husband is doing? This will hurt our family, and it doesn't seem like You are doing anything about it. So I need to do something until You shake some sense into his head." Peace will come when we are content to wait for God to move in HIS way and time. Philippians 4:6-7 says, "Do not be anxious about anything, but in every situation, by prayer and petition, with thanksgiving, present your requests to God. And the peace of God, which transcends all understanding, will guard your hearts and your minds in Christ Jesus." (Philippians 4:6-7 NKJV)

Joy comes through submission in marriage. God will take care of your needs more while submitting. God will begin to show your husband where he is neglecting your needs. When you obey God, He moves in beautiful ways. Psalm 16:11 says, "You make known to me the path of life; in your presence, there is fullness of joy; at your right hand are pleasures forevermore." (Psalm 16:11 ESV)

Hope also comes through submission in marriage. When you see God move, it grows your hope and faith that God will move again! Obeying God always leads to abundant blessings and true freedom. God will restore your marriage just like He did in Judah and Jerusalem. Jeremiah 33:6 says "But now take another look. I'm going to give this city a thorough renovation, working true healing inside and out. I will show them life, whole, life brimming with blessings. I'll restore everything that was lost to Judah and Jerusalem. I'll build everything back as good as new." (Jeremiah 33:6 MSG)

Chapter 4

How to Walk in Your Superpower

As women, we must understand how God designed us to walk in our God-given power. As with anything, when we don't use a product for its intended use, we will destroy it. Just like I can't heat my bath water with my curling iron, I can't make my marriage work without the right tools used in the right way. It is vital for women to be aware of the need for their husbands to feel like a hero and how to trigger this instinct in them for them to commit to you and love you forever.

So, what is a Hero? A hero is someone everyone admires and looks up to for being brave and doing great things for others. They are the person who always saves the day—someone who shows no fear and is beyond skilled. Think about the Marvel Superhero franchises—most men love those movies because they identify with the hero. In a certain respect, we all want to feel like heroes. However, the difference between men and women is that men need to feel heroic, and women like to be the hero, but it's not necessary for them. Women's favorite movies usually have a male hero at the end protecting the woman he loves.

God has given women a superpower through our attitude, behavior, and sexuality. We have the power to empower our husbands.

We can start the transformation we want in our marriages today when we understand how our husbands are naturally designed by God. God illustrates this by comparing marriage to Christ and the church.

Marriage is Like Christ and the Church

Christ is the head and the Savior of the church; just like the husband is the head and savior of the wife. In this context of the husband saving the wife, this means he puts her first in all matters (i.e. she drives the best car, she gets the new dress, and he cares about what she thinks). He cherishes her, loves her and puts her first, takes care of her financially, defends her in front of others and cares for her like his own body, as Christ does the church. Christ is the Hero of all Heroes, just like the husband needs to be the hero of the wife. Men are designed by God to need our honor, to be our protection, and to be the head of the household, just like Christ is the Head of the church. Jesus loved the church so much, He died for it. Ephesians 5:22-30 says, "Wives, be subject (be submissive and adapt yourselves) to your own husbands as [a service] to the Lord. For the husband is head of the wife as Christ is the Head of the church, Himself the Savior of [His] body. As the church is subject to Christ, so let wives also be subject in everything to their husbands. Husbands, love your wives, as Christ loved the church and gave Himself up for her, so that He might sanctify her, having cleansed her by the washing of water with the Word, that He might present the church to Himself in glorious splendor, without spot or wrinkle or any such things [that she might be holy and faultless].

Even so, husbands should love their wives as [being in a sense] their own bodies. He who loves his own wife loves himself. For no man ever hated his own flesh but nourishes and carefully protects and cherishes it, as Christ does the church, because we are members (parts) of His body. For this reason, a man shall leave his father and his mother and shall be joined to his wife, and the two shall become one flesh. (Ephesians 5:22-30 AMPC)

Let's take a look at this. Every man has been called by God to be the head and leader of his home. However, to effectively fulfill his role, a man needs support from his wife. A wife can provide this support by honoring, respecting, and trusting her husband's leadership abilities. Although mistakes will be made, it is important to give your husband the space and time needed and allow God to grow and develop him into the leader and husband that God called him to be for YOU. There may be times when you fear your husband's decision-making abilities or worry about being taken advantage of. You might even feel that your husband is undeserving of respect and honor.
However, when you choose to honor your husband as a **service** to God, then God is obligated to reward you.

What is the Purpose of Treating Him Like a Hero?

As a wife, you must be your husband's biggest supporter and cheerleader, treating him like a hero. Encourage him to lead well and help him overcome his fears. Although he may not admit it due to his masculinity, a man's greatest fear is often failing to lead his family. Men desire to be the hero and want their wives to be happy. Men hate conflict, which often stems from criticism, debate, and arguments; all of these are indicators to them that they are not heroic, which goes against how they were designed.

Although men are designed to be heroes, that doesn't mean wives cannot talk to their husbands about everything and be heard; remember, we are a team. Relationships are about discussion; two people are freely talking and expressing how they feel without persuasion, manipulation, and anger. As a wife, you are anointed by God and have been given the power to nurture not only your children, but also your husband.

As mothers, we often put all our energy and attention into our children, trying to help them be their best. We do this because we want to feel validated and prove to ourselves that we are good parents.
However, in doing so, we often forget about ourselves and our husbands, losing ourselves in living through our children, which should be second and not first.
We often forget that our children are influenced by many voices and may grow up to have values and beliefs different from what we've instilled in them.

One thing is sure: our children will become independent and start living their own lives by going to college or starting a family. This means they will want to create their own family traditions, which may not include their parents. If we haven't built a strong love connection with our husbands, we will feel lonely and disappointed. We may even end up getting a divorce after being together for many years, simply because we don't know each other well enough apart from our children.

Nurturing does not mean treating your husband like one of the children, telling him what to do, and when to come and go. Nurturing is also not financially taking care of your husband if he does not work. Of course, if your husband loses his job or gets injured, you should be there to support and encourage him. However, he should get another job ASAP; the job doesn't have to be in his field! If you don't have a job, you don't have a field. Remember, the hero wants to take care of you. To nurture our husbands simply means to provide them with support and encouragement.

Women today think they will be happy if they have control in their marriages. When a wife grows impatient with her husband and takes charge by making all of the decisions and plans, she may think she has won, but in reality, she has lost. Disempowering her husband instead of empowering him may cause him to be disengaged and passive, or passive-aggressive. In either case, the wife's needs will not be met, and she will feel more lonely than ever.

If your husband becomes passive, more than likely, he will not embrace or engage in the relationship. He has given up, so you will have to make all the decisions, parent the children alone, or feel like he's just another child, which can hurt intimacy and be a sexual turn-off for many women.

If your husband becomes passive-aggressive, more than likely, you will feel alone, as he has stopped communicating with you. You may feel insecure because he makes sarcastic remarks, and you may feel confused because he allows things to build up without confronting them. He reaches his maximum point and then explodes and becomes aggressive.

If this is the current state of your marriage, it's time to examine your trust, honor, and respect towards your husband. Are you allowing him to lead the family?

When wives initiate honor and respect for their husbands, the husband will automatically begin to fulfill his responsibility as the head of the home, by leading and caring for his wife with a servant leadership attitude. Think of this analogy: you can have a beautiful, luxury car, but without fuel, the car is useless. Women are the fuel for the car to run; the car cannot run without the fuel. The better the fuel (initiating honor and respect for your husband), the better the car runs. I use 93 octane, super-premium! This is why the scripture says we have the power to build or tear down because it all starts with us... the wife! Proverbs 14:1-4 NLT says, "A wise woman builds her home, but a foolish woman tears it down with her own hands. Those who follow the right path fear the Lord; those who take the wrong path despise him. A fool's proud talk becomes a rod that beats him, but the words of the wise keep them safe." (Proverbs 14:1-4 NLT)

We may feel like we are on the back burner when we initiate honor and respect for our husbands, even when it is not deserved. I know what you are thinking. Why do I have to initiate it? He's the head. Because God made the wife the helper and completer of her husband, and God is trying to get something to you: to be cherished by your husband and to realize the power that He has given to you as a woman. When you choose to do it God's way, you're now walking in your superpower because you've allowed your husband to grow and develop, without fear, into his manhood. NOW, your husband wants nothing more than to please you, and your every wish becomes his command because a woman's power is subtle and undeniable. The relationship becomes effortless, because your husband will want to please you all of the time! Isaiah 1:19 KJV says, "If ye be willing and obedient, ye shall eat the good of the land." (Isaiah 1:19 KJV)

Real Beauty is Inner Beauty

The earlier years of my marriage and years of marriage counseling have only solidified my belief that inner beauty is not only necessary but also the key ingredient and the profound truth to a happy, great marriage because when you develop inner beauty, it's an unfading beauty that can not only capture your husband's heart forever, but cause him to become a believer of Jesus Christ!

63

According to 1 Peter, even if our husband is unequally yoked (an unbeliever or spiritually immature), our behavior and pure reverence can still win him over even when the Word doesn't work. Now that's power! Go ahead, Superwoman! The scripture emphasizes that it's not our words ("much discussion"), beauty, clothes, or jewelry that win them over, but our godly behavior.

 1 Peter 3:1-5 says, "Wives, in the same way, submit yourselves to your own husbands so that, if any of them do not believe the word, they may be won over without words by the behavior of their wives, when they see the purity and reverence of your lives. Your beauty should not come from outward adornment, such as elaborate hairstyles and the wearing of gold jewelry or fine clothes. Rather, it should be that of your inner self, the unfading beauty of a gentle and quiet spirit, which is of great worth in God's sight. For this is the way the holy women of the past who put their hope in God used to adorn themselves. (1 Peter 3:1-5 NIV)

Today, we tend to prioritize our sexuality rather than honoring God with our words and conduct, but true inner beauty is built through having good character. Some women have become masculine and are losing their femininity, which only a woman can provide. Inner beauty is what men can't resist — inner beauty never fades, no matter how our bodies may change. Your husband may glance at another woman, but his heart will always belong to you. When women surrender their lives to God, God gives them a revelation of their true superpower.

These days, we want everything — before we can afford them. Things we don't need like designer clothes, bags, and luxury cars; we often bypass our husbands and the team to get what we want when we want it. Then, when we are in over our heads and want to be rescued by our hero and he doesn't show up, we are upset and claim he isn't worth two pennies.

Don't get me wrong, I like nice things, too, but I never forget that stuff comes and goes, not my commitment to building my life on God's design. I now have nice things and my husband's love, too. Okay, I know what you're thinking. If I ever need help, I'll just work overtime, get a second job, or cut back on other expenses to compensate for the financial shortages. If you do that, you unconsciously establish a precedent with this choice and may be unaware of the implications. Your husband may depend on you to solve the problems, making him feel less like a hero and it will ruin the intimacy of being taken care of. What I love the most about marriage is the security and safety I feel. I don't have to worry about anything — Nick will take care of it.

Nothing is worse than a bitter and resentful woman trying to navigate life alone because she is so insecure and afraid to give love that she operates with an independent spirit. As a strong woman, your role is to support your husband by letting him know how thankful and appreciative you are; he is taking care of you and the family. I know you work, too. However, there are so many women having the task of doing it all to make ends meet. Most likely she ends up in this position because she used her superpower the wrong way. It is easier to persuade your husband with a polite attitude rather than with rude demands and negativity. You can catch more bees with honey than with vinegar.

A man feels more empowered and more loved than ever when he feels like a hero. He will spread all his love to you because he knows you are the only one who gives him the wind beneath his wings. Everyone wants to be loved, supported, and cared for, so stop buying into the rhetoric of the world's system and use your superpower God's way.

Chapter 5

Good Women vs. Godly Women

We are going to explore a pivotal difference in the way we do things. We have convinced ourselves that our good deeds should give us what we want in our marriage, and we find ourselves bitter and offended when it doesn't go how we expected. During the earlier years of my marriage, I was this woman, and I couldn't understand why all my good deeds did not make my husband stay home or cause him to appreciate and cherish me. When we see someone being good or doing good deeds, we automatically assume God is pleased with them. However, reading Romans 12 shows us it's not just about good deeds, but about our hearts. As the old saying goes, "A man that grades his own test has a fool for a teacher."

Do it 'Cause You Love Me

I want to share a story from the early years of my marriage to Nick. I will use Romans chapter 12 throughout the story to illustrate the difference between what I thought I should do, versus what the Word of God says I should do in this situation. I share these stories because I want you to see it's a process that requires thoughtfulness and guidance from the Holy Spirit because God's word may not align with our initial human response.

Many of you will identify with my responses and reasoning, but I want you to understand it's not so much about right and wrong; it's about honoring God.

We cannot respond like the world and expect God's blessings. Romans 12:2 says, "Do not be conformed to this world (this age), [fashioned after and adapted to its external, superficial customs], but be transformed (changed) by the [entire] renewal of your mind [by its new ideals and its new attitude], so that you may prove [for yourselves] what is the good and acceptable and perfect will of God, even the thing which is good and acceptable and perfect [in His sight for you]." (Romans 12:2 AMPC)

I spent the first few years of my marriage as a homemaker, taking care of our children, cooking, cleaning, and asking Nick to handle any home repairs or maintenance I couldn't manage. He ignored me or said he would do it later, and on top of that, he would stay out two and three days at a time, which made me furious. One particular day, as I prepared to confront him, I started to reflect on my behavior. When I looked inside myself, I recognized that my behavior had been far from perfect, and why would he want to come home to that?

As a committed Christian, I knew I wasn't supposed to return evil for evil, but I didn't know that loving my husband unconditionally would lead him to realize his mistakes and change. Romans 12:21 says, "Do not let yourself be overcome by evil, but overcome (master) evil with good." (Romans 12:21 AMPC)

It was hard for me to love him that way because he didn't deserve it. I would barely talk to him, isolate myself, fix his plate, and leave and go to my room, still thinking I was being a submitted wife because of my good deeds. If he asked me a question, the answer was short; that was my way of punishing him. It was my way of standing up for myself. I knew I wouldn't leave, and God hated divorce, so I figured that behavior was the best way to get the message across. It was the only way I could make Nick understand that his behavior was unacceptable. Romans 12:20 says, "But if your enemy is hungry, feed him; if he is thirsty, give him drink; for by doing so you will heap burning coals upon his head." (Romans 12:20 AMPC)

Now, I know that seems extreme, but hear me! If God says to do that for your enemy, what should you do for the one you claim to love? A godly wife knows she can turn her husband's heart towards her with true kindness. Romans 12:14 says, "Bless those who persecute you [who are cruel in their attitude toward you]; bless and do not curse them." (Romans 12:14 AMPC)

Sometimes, if he had a bad attitude toward me, I would be ready to fight and say provoking things because I couldn't believe he would have the audacity to be angry with me when he was out doing God knows what. Being a woman, my first thought was he was cheating; even though Nick assured me there was no other woman, I didn't believe him. A couple of times, I followed him without his knowledge and would find him with his buddies in the gambling hall all night. I was relieved it wasn't another woman, but I found another concerning issue explaining our financial problems. Nick had a serious gambling addiction. I used to tell myself, "You are a Christian — you shouldn't get angry, you should show love." One time we started arguing, I heard a voice in the room say, "Do it because you love me." It was so loud in my spirit that I thought I heard it with my natural ears. It stopped me in my tracks. I looked around the room. I knew it was God because no one else was in the room with us. I said, "Yes, Lord," in my heart. Romans 12:12 says, "Rejoice and exult in hope; be steadfast and patient in suffering and tribulation; be constant in prayer." (Romans 12:12 AMPC)

When I got angry with Nick, God would remind me, "Do it because you love Me." God wanted me to love Nick unconditionally, not through works or good deeds, but through grace, in the same way God loves me. My performance has nothing to do with God's love for me. We receive God's love through believing in Jesus the Savior; we did nothing to deserve or earn it.
I want you to understand that your feelings are valid!

However, God wants you to do things with humility and with a cheerful heart. Doing and saying things from a place of spite and bragging can turn your husband away from God. My words were causing a rebellious spirit in my husband, pushing him to continue to behave in a way he already knew was wrong.

God prompted me not to worry about what Nick was doing anymore. I wasn't going to let another day go by being upset about his gambling addiction and him staying out all night. I prayed and enjoyed life with my children. After my encounter with God, I could withstand Nick's behavior because I was doing it for God. As I surrendered to God, I could cast my care on Him. Nick's gambling addiction and his schedule didn't bother me anymore. I had heard from God! I was at peace and walking in joy in the midst of trouble. God began to grow my husband and showed him how his gambling addiction was hurting his family and the call of God on his life. God began to stir my husband's heart to care about how his gambling habits and busy schedule were impacting our well-being and causing insecurity in our children and me, all without me saying a word. Nick came home one day and said he was going back to church. That next Sunday, he woke up early, got dressed, and prepared to attend church. From that point on, our lives changed and were never the same. We grew closer in the things of God, and the blessings of the Lord overtook our lives. Let go and let God! When you obey God, He will favor you and reward you! So I now began to understand why my good deeds did not produce anything because I thought submission was only about doing a good deed, but it's about the heart in which we do it. There is a difference between a good woman and a godly woman. Let's look at the defining characteristics of two women. The godly woman, the Proverbs 31 woman, is often defined by what she does and her title. It's more important to look deeper into her character and who she is to be inspired by her example. The good woman may appear godly in her actions, but the difference is in her attitude and character. Her "godliness" is performative and not genuine, and she expects her reward from others, not God. I don't want to list a godly woman's characteristics to condemn you or make you feel less. I want to dive into the details so you can understand the difference between godly and good, to encourage you that the Proverbs 31 woman isn't some unattainable goal, but a change of heart towards the Father. God wants more than imitation from his daughters. Proverbs 21:2 says, "Every man's way is right in his own eyes, But the Lord weighs and examines the hearts [of people and their motives]." (Proverbs 21:2 AMPC)

"Good" Versus "Godly" Characteristics

- A good woman wants to fit in. However, she is insecure and compares herself to other women.

- A godly woman knows her value, is aware of her worth, and celebrates her differences.

- A good woman needs many possessions to feel valued, so she spends money according to her emotions and doesn't save any money for emergencies.

- A godly woman is financially competent and is confident with or without money: She knows when to save and when to spend.

- A good woman, when she is hurt, is quick to anger; you must be careful what you say and how you say it. She will "get you," "tell you off," or "read you," and that ain't no cap!

- A godly woman is not dangerous and isn't aggressive, even if she is offended.

- A good woman brings stress to her marriage because she is needy. She complains often, which drives her husband to spend time with his boys versus spending time with her.

- A godly woman brings more to her marriage than money. She brings benefits to her husband in ways neither his money nor his friends can provide. That's part of her magnetism and why her husband must be near her and cherishes her.

- A good woman works, but complains to her husband, and prioritizes shopping and focusing on social media over working.

- A godly woman enjoys her work and works willingly.

- A good woman may quit her job because she doesn't like it and doesn't care about how it affects the family.

- A godly woman understands and embraces change and the need for variety in the home, but not at the expense of her family's stability. She sees the bigger picture.

- A good woman may not support her husband's idea when she doesn't agree with it and may even try to sabotage the plan. She is not flexible, adaptable, or adjustable.

- A godly woman contributes and cooperates even when things don't go her way. She's adaptable, rolls with the punches, and doesn't whine or complain about changing her plan.

- A good woman may be insecure, so she gossips about others to make herself feel better.

- A godly woman doesn't look down on anyone; she is compassionate and happy to serve.

The beautiful part about Romans 12 and Proverbs 31 is that our good deeds cannot move our husbands to love and cherish us. Instead, it's our unconditional love for them that moves them. The hardest part of solving a problem is identifying its root cause. It's not that you aren't DOING enough; you need to do it with the right heart and motive. God rewards our obedience, not our good deeds.

Chapter 6

Empower Your Man and Get Your Needs Met

We have talked about several key points. I want to take this next section to illustrate how treating your man like a hero and being a godly wife go hand-in-hand with getting YOUR needs met!

I think it is fair to say that most people go into marriage with high expectations of their spouse or thinking their spouse is the same as them. We have accepted this notion that our spouse completes us. To that point, I will say this: God has given you everything you need to be a whole and complete human, and no other person can complete you. When I married, I believed it was Nick's responsibility to make me happy, which is impossible! No one can always make you happy. People can't even make themselves happy every day. We can't put that responsibility on someone else; that's wrong. You're responsible for your own happiness; in the same regard, you are responsible for what you allow to upset you. We, as women, have more control over this aspect of our marriage than we realize.

I can hear you now, "But Pastor Frannie, this is supposed to be about my needs as a woman!" Yes, women have needs. But often, their needs aren't being met for two reasons:
First, we don't understand the needs of our husbands. Men and women are not only different physically, but mentally as well.

Men's needs are different from women's needs. When men are preoccupied with work or money, women interpret it as rejection. You may think your husband may not want to be around you, but one of the basic needs of a man is financial independence and status.

Secondly, our needs are not being met because we are not adequately communicating our needs to our spouse. Assuming your husband will know when you are tired and need a break from the routine can often lead to resentment. You become upset because you think he should realize you are exhausted. However, some men are so obsessed with achieving financial goals; they may not even notice you are tired and need a break because they are also tired from doing mental gymnastics thinking about how to make money all day. So, it's important to communicate what you need clearly. For instance, if you need a break, ask your husband to put the kids to bed and order dinner. This will help both parties avoid misunderstandings and ensure everyone's needs are met.

Investing into a Great Marriage

So why did I spend so much time acting as my husband's cheerleader? Because I love him and always wanted him to enjoy being married to me. Selfishness is a common cause of broken marriages and women failing to respect, encourage, and admire their husbands. Men need to know they are appreciated; they appreciate compliments just as much as women do.

Let's take a look at seven areas that describe what a man needs from his wife and what a woman needs from her husband. You will see that these go hand in hand! Consider making an investment and trust that God will bring you a return.

1. So you want to be number one, right? Do you want to feel you are more important than your husband's business or job and significantly more important than his mother, children, friends, sports, and hobbies? When a woman doesn't try to fix, change, or "mother" her husband, she creates an environment where he can be himself. When you respect your husband by letting him be a man and being who he was designed to be without the need to fix him, he will drop the remote stuck on ESPN, come out of his cave more often, hand you his heart, and engage you emotionally....without losing his masculinity.

2. Let's say you and your husband get into a heated argument. Sometimes, the tendency is for a woman to push for instant conflict resolution (demanding answers right away, criticizing their behavior). What's going on in your man's mind is totally the opposite. He's going, "I need some space now!" Proverbs 21:9 says, "It is better to dwell in a corner of the housetop [on the flat oriental roof, exposed to all kinds of weather] than in a house shared with a nagging, quarrelsome, and faultfinding woman." (Proverbs 21:9 AMPC) Giving him the time and space to process his thoughts in his way is essential. Let him express himself and vent his frustrations when he's ready. Men appreciate your advice

77

and criticism when it is requested. Remember, men are designed to be the hero. This is how the wife starts genuine intimacy flowing because he doesn't feel pressured to communicate at that time. As a result, he will be excited to spend time with you, he will start to compliment you more, and even help you around the house.

3. You must always maintain your integrity! When your husband sees that your integrity and trust in God can't be compromised, it will also grow his trust in you. He will begin to demonstrate character, integrity, and become a trustworthy man. He will trust that you have his best interest at heart, and when you speak, he will listen.

4. Be attractive and grow your inner beauty. The attraction that a mature man desires goes beyond the physical and into the emotional. Men desire a woman with inner beauty. Inner beauty is when you can release shame, depression, anger, sadness, and fear. That means a woman's love for self, her passion for life, and how she carries herself will transcend his love for her. Your husband will begin to connect with you at your best, and sparks will fly. You will experience true intimacy and connection in your marriage.

5. Understanding and expressing love in your husband's preferred love language is important. The term "love language" refers to a person's preferred way of communicating and receiving love. Your husband's love language could be one of the following: words of affirmation, quality time, gifts, acts of service, or physical touch.

You can take "The 5 Love Languages Assessment" https://5lovelanguages.com/quizzes/love-language by Gary Chapman to find out your husband's love language. It will help you understand how to express love in a way that your husband can receive it. Similarly, your husband can take the same assessment to discover how to love in the way you receive it. You can maintain a happy and healthy relationship by keeping your husband's love tank filled with his preferred love language.

6. It's important for a wife to connect with her husband on various levels, not just the ones that have an emotional connection with her. Show appreciation for all aspects of your husband because you care for him. Take an interest in things that he likes and compliment him often. If you value his appearance, leadership abilities, or his initiative in fixing things around the house, let him know how much you appreciate it. By doing so, he will begin to truly share his life with you, love and accept you for who you are, and think that you are the most beautiful woman in the world.

7. Respect him by offering yourself for physical affection (yes, sex). When a wife willingly and passionately initiates lovemaking with her husband, it demonstrates respect for his need for physical affection, which is when a man feels the most loved by his wife. In return, he will meet your need for affection, to be tenderly held, and to be near you, apart from times of sexual intimacy.

Overview of the Differences Between Men and Women

MEN	WOMEN
Men feel devastated by failure and financial setbacks; they tend to obsess about money much more than women.	Women are very concerned about issues relating to physical attractiveness. Changes in this area can be as difficult for women as changes in a man's financial status.
Men are motivated when they feel needed. A man's deepest fear is that he is not good enough or not competent enough, though he may never express this.	Women are motivated when they feel special or cherished. A woman's sense of self is defined through the quality of her relationships.
Men rarely talk about their problems unless they are seeking "expert" advice; asking for help when you can do something yourself is a sign of weakness.	For women, offering help is not a sign of weakness, but a sign of strength; it is a sign of caring to give support.
Men avoid housework and try to get others to do it at all costs. They feel demeaned by doing it because it doesn't feel heroic.	Women view the cleanliness of the house as a manifestation of a warm, cozy nest. Men have a different threshold for cleanliness than women do.

MEN	WOMEN
Men often feel responsible or feel they're to blame for women's problems.	Women often feel they're not enough or at fault when the marital relationship is not going well.
Men have a much more difficult time relating to their own feelings and may feel very threatened by the expression of feelings in their presence. This may cause them to react by withdrawing or attempting to control the situation through a display of control and/or power.	Women are in touch with a much wider range of feelings than men, and the intensity of those feelings is usually much greater for women than men. As a result of this, many men perceive that women's feelings appear to change quickly; men may find this irrational and difficult to understand.

As you can see, there are significant differences between men and women. These differences are not better or worse. Do not judge the differences, try to change them, or make them go away; it will only make things worse. To operate as a team and get along, it is important to respect these differences. Keep these differences in mind while communicating about anything important, expressing care and concern, or resolving conflicts. To empower your man and fulfill your needs, it is important to understand the differences between men and women and to renew your mind. This involves not only gathering godly information but also adopting God's way of thinking and applying it to your life. Proverbs 4:7 says, "Wisdom is the principal thing; therefore get wisdom: and with all thy getting, get understanding." (Proverbs 4:7 KJV)

Chapter 7

Communication

Effective communication is a skill that can be applied in every area of life. If you can master the art of communication in your marriage, it will flow naturally into your relationships with your children, co-workers, family members, etc. This is an area that everyone can benefit from and we all should be aware of common communication pitfalls.

The benefit of proper communication is that everyone feels heard. In marriage counseling, we often hear, "I just don't feel heard." And when your partner doesn't feel heard, they don't feel loved or respected. It's important that we genuinely listen to our spouses. Learning to compromise is essential when it comes to good communication. Give and take is what it's all about. Robust and healthy communication helps promote intimacy and bring feelings of safety and security into your marriage.

What are Some of the Barriers to Effective Communication?

- Selfishness
- Pride
- Low self-esteem
- Self-preservation
- Tit-for-tat behavior
- Trauma
- Lack of respect
- Lack of education
- Not understanding the audience
- Learning and processing disabilities

The key to effective communication is recognizing that barriers exist and discussing how to get past them with your spouse. When you can share difficulties and work together to find a path forward, your relationship will go to the next level. Poor listeners interrupt; they do not listen and just try to get their point across. Another sign of poor communication is looking outward, not asking the right questions, or being thoughtless and defensive. We don't want this kind of behavior as we're getting aligned in our marriage — we want to learn how to listen and be heard effectively in marriage.

Upbringing and culture often influence the way people communicate. As someone in an interracial marriage, I've noticed this firsthand.

My husband, Nick, is Italian-American, a culture known for being loud and expressive about their thoughts. They tend to speak their minds without hesitation. I'm African-American and was raised by older, religious parents who taught me to keep my matters private. As a result, I was more reserved and quiet.

When Nick and I first started dating, I noticed that he was very affectionate towards me. He would hug and hold me frequently, which was uncomfortable because I grew up in a household where I saw my parents kiss only once. I don't recall seeing my parents hardly ever showing physical affection to each other. It was always kept private.

Nick and I often disagreed on how to parent our children. Nick wanted the kids to run freely while I tried to protect them from potential dangers we couldn't see. As a parent, knowing where your children are is important. That's why I preferred them to play in front of the house instead of two streets away, which is how I was raised. In the 90s, we didn't have cell phones or GPS devices, so setting and enforcing boundaries was critical to ensure my kids' safety.

As Nick got into the Word of God, our communication slowly improved. We decided that if it wasn't a kingdom issue, meaning something that went against the Word of God, then it wasn't worth arguing about.

How to Have Effective Conversations

To have a productive conversation, it's important to have a clear idea of what you hope to achieve. Starting with a solid foundation will allow you to focus on the areas that can improve your relationship. Here are three straightforward steps to help you become a more effective communicator.

1. Check yourself and understand your motivation. Ensure that you are adding value rather than causing harm to your spouse. Agreement with your spouse is more important than being right, even if you believe you are correct.

2. Communicate at the right time. Consider whether this is the appropriate time, place, and audience for the conversation.

3. Prepare to win. Communicate to learn, validate, and be prepared to compromise.

Today, the most significant missing ingredient in marriage is compromising. Amid widespread selfishness, compromising is crucial to foster a prosperous marriage. You must genuinely care about the other person's thoughts and feelings to achieve authentic communication and a desire to move the ball forward in your marriage.

We often experience communication failures in everyday situations. One spouse may approach a conversation in a way that seems rational and logical, but this approach can be perceived as lacking empathy and displaying a condescending attitude toward the other spouse.

This 'logical' communicator often acts like this:
- They offer resolutions that are so reasonable that one might wonder how anyone could see it differently.
- They provide logical answers.
- They calmly explain anything that you may have a question about.
- They take pride in their logic and intelligence and do not display emotions.
- When someone shows emotions, they calmly wait until the other person's emotions subside before responding logically.
- They show no empathy.

But this dispassionate approach doesn't work for everyone. We must recognize that our spouses should be approached with empathy, rather than as a logic puzzle.

Another common pitfall is being ready to play the Blame Game. Trying to find someone to blame is a master course in manipulation. The worst part about this is that it's not about a resolution or an answer to the issue. It's solely about shifting blame and responsibility.

For example, the "You" statement. "It's all YOUR fault; if YOU had listened to me..." Blaming others is a common habit for those who tend to be authoritative and may resort to verbal abuse to get their way. They suffer from low self-esteem and have difficulty admitting when they're wrong. It's important to take responsibility for our actions instead of blaming others.

Effective communication is vital in promoting a healthy and satisfying marriage, especially when resolving conflicts. When both partners feel heard and understood, the relationship can thrive. It is essential to remember that communication aims to find the best outcome for everyone, not just one person. Couples can strengthen their intimacy, lower their emotional barriers, and establish a sense of safety and security by learning to compromise and communicate in healthy ways.

Communication will improve with your spouse as you obey God. It's important to acknowledge when we are wrong and confess our past mistakes, as this process will change our relationship with our spouse. Many times, it can be difficult to understand and get to the heart of what a person is saying. However, you can ask God for wisdom and He will reveal their heart to you. James 1:5 says, "If any of you is deficient in wisdom, let him ask of the giving God [Who gives] to everyone liberally and ungrudgingly, without reproaching or faultfinding, and it will be given him." (James 1:5 AMPC) Remember, this is a journey and it requires effort, but the end result is worth it.

Chapter 8

Vision

So far, we've talked about love connections and how to set the scene for a fantastic marriage that brings you fulfillment and joy. My goal is to help you get the answers you need.

I began to see a common thread in marriages: a need for a shared vision. Having a shared vision is one of the most powerful things we can do to enhance our relationships. When couples are not aligned on their goals and aspirations for the future, it can lead to misunderstandings, conflicts, disconnections, and even divorce.

Shared vision is something you discover together. It involves alignment, agreement, support, and service to others and should be clearly communicated and understood. Having a shared vision in marriage provides a template and a roadmap for success. I'm talking about a godly and not a worldly vision because the Bible says something specific about a godly vision. Proverbs 29:18 says, "Where there is no vision [no redemptive revelation of God], the people perish; but he who keeps the law [of God, which includes that of man]—blessed (happy, fortunate, and enviable) is he." (Proverbs 29:18 AMPC)

In the past, my husband Nick and I lacked direction and stability in our marriage. We reached a point where all our belongings were crammed in a 26-foot U-Haul trailer parked in my mother's driveway, and we were living in one bedroom of her house. This situation left us in a destitute state. Despite earning six figures our finances had no clear purpose, vision, or mission. As a result, our financial situation ultimately collapsed. Nick would watch Pastor Dollar on TV at night and was intrigued by the prosperity message. Nick and I were always perplexed about how we could attend church every Sunday, yet our lives remained unchanged. We were tithers, but we did not understand the attitude in which you tithe that makes the difference in your harvest. We tithed out of duty because we knew it was something we were supposed to do instead of tithing from a cheerful and thankful heart. 2 Corinthians 9:6-8 says, "Remember this: Whoever sows sparingly will also reap sparingly, and whoever sows generously will also reap generously. Each of you should give what you have decided in your heart to give, not reluctantly or under compulsion, for God loves a cheerful giver. And God is able to bless you abundantly, so that in all things at all times, having all that you need, you will abound in every good work." (2 Corinthians 9:6-8 NIV)

Nick and I had a lot to do to renew our minds (exchange our thoughts for God's thoughts) and activate faith in our lives. So we started on our journey. At Revealing Truth Ministries (RTM), we were being taught things we had never seen in the Bible before, and we started to see results in our lives. We didn't understand the concept of vision, but we learned if we submit to another man's vision, God would grace us with our own. Luke 16:12 says, "And if ye have not been faithful in that which is another man's, who shall give you that which is your own?" (Luke 16:12 KJV)

90

We were also taught at RTM, the importance of serving God and having a godly vision. The Bible asks, "How can two walk together unless they agree?" When Nick ran his own business, he managed our finances like a shell game, which left me confused about where the money was going. As a result, Pastor Powe told Nick to shut down his business, and find a regular job, which led to a significant decrease in our household income. However, by taking a job that provided a steady paycheck, Nick could be more accountable to me, which set us on the path of getting our life in order according to God's Word. Until there is order, there can't be any increase. God revealed the absolute Truth, through our pastors. If we do not heed biblical instructions, we will not experience prosperity and peace. Hebrew 13:17 says, "Obey your [spiritual] leaders and submit to them [recognizing their authority over you], for they are keeping watch over your souls and continually guarding your spiritual welfare as those who will give an account [of their stewardship of you]. Let them do this with joy and not with grief and groans, for this would be of no benefit to you."
(Hebrew 13:17 AMP)

Vision is about oneness. The shared vision for your family could be as simple as "Supporting your pastors" or "Serving in your local church." The vision has to be clear, relevant, and significant. If the vision is a calling to the five-fold ministry gifts (apostle, prophet, evangelist, pastor, and teacher), your husband may not have all the details, so as a wife, don't get frustrated; it's okay not to have all the answers. Women want the details of where, when, and how. It makes us feel secure. But we should trust the Holy Spirit to lead and guide us along the way.

I know what you are thinking, "Honey, what about my vision?" Be patient; you will discover yours in his, because you are one. While serving in ministry with Nick, I discovered one of my purposes was to write this book, something I never thought in a million years I would do!

Women, when you submit to God, He won't let you fail. He will always take care of you and bring you out on top. He will not put anything on you that you can't bear. Don't try to sit down and create some strategy, business plan, and grandiose vision for your family.

This is why it's paramount to find a church and a pastor to submit to, serve that vision, and allow God to guide you to the purpose that He created you for; this purpose was created before the foundation of the world — the vision God wants for you and your family will become clear if you let it.

Vision eliminates distractions. If you feel lost in your marriage, decide today to submit to a vision because submitting to a vision together will bring your marriage into unity. As you read this book, think about what you're believing God to do in your marriage. Be honest and get out of your comfort zone with this so you can connect authentically to God's-given purpose for you and your family. A shared vision in marriage is the ultimate devil killer and brings alignment. There is nothing more important to God than marriage. Marriage is the central theme of the Bible and is about God, family, and unity.

Shared Vision and the Local Church

It's important to understand the role of your local church and connect with a shared vision to create alignment in your marriage. I want to detail my personal story with you to emphasize this point.

When Nick and I arrived at RTM, God was moving us toward alignment in our marriage. Pastor Powe started teaching a sermon series titled "The Righteousness of God," which challenged my previous beliefs, my understanding of how God worked, and everything I built my worth and knowledge on. I realized that I had been living under the Law and not under the grace of Jesus. Pastor Powe would read scriptures that said my worldly sinner husband was on the same footing as me! Me - the woman who grew up in the church since she was five and sacrificed greatly to be a good Christian, mom, and wife. My personal value was tossed out in one sermon. It was devastating. Especially when I saw how Nick took to it like a fish in water, hanging onto every word Pastor Powe said, and receiving it without hesitation.

Meanwhile, I'm drowning in my own knowledge and religion. My church upbringing was full of fire and brimstone; we were taught to be sin-conscious.

As a child, I remember making sure I did all the "do's" and avoided all the "don'ts". I didn't curse, I didn't steal, I didn't lie, I dressed modestly, pleased my parents, served in my dad's church - my entire almost 40 years now was spent observing the law to the best of my ability. So, to come to this point after all that, to hear that religion was wrong, was very difficult. The songs we sang and I grew up listening to like, "Lord, I'm running trying to make a 100 cause 99 and a half, won't do" or "I'm climbing the rough side of the mountain, doing my best to make it in" emphasized that law.

I had to pray and ask God to help me understand Pastor Powe's teaching. I remember sitting on the edge of my seat in service, holding back tears and looking to be sure every scripture Pastor Powe gave us was in context. I was shocked. How could I have served so long and missed so much? I would ask God, "What am I doing wrong here? I've been doing my best to make it in since I was a little child." Meanwhile, Pastor Powe is taking Nick under his wing. Nick is flying on the private jet, going on ministry trips with him, and driving the Pastor around in the golf cart in the church's parking lot, while Pastor Powe greeted the people.

Nick is walking into the things of God just like a walk in the park, happy, free, and PREACHING TO ME — the Saint! How dare he? I was happy to see him moving forward in Christ with a highly respected pastor; it was an answered prayer. But I was unwilling to hear anything about the Bible and Jesus from Nick!

Keep in mind I was with Nick for 15 years of him messing it up, so I wasn't ready to be preached to by a heathen. I was the responsible one, I grew up in the church, I received God at five years old. There was no way Nick was ahead of me in the knowledge of the Word. Seeing him walk in and be received by the pastor made me jealous. I wanted to see him tarry and repent, to suffer for his wrongdoings and apologize to me. Soon, I found myself offended because it was not fair.

I wanted what Nick had, that peace and freedom, that intuitive sense of worthiness. I asked God to reveal it to me, and God started to reveal my heart. The Holy Spirit asked me, "Why wouldn't you want Nick to get it?" Then I began to see that this wasn't about Nick; this was about my heart. I saw that I was the dirty one. Clearly, I had misunderstood. It wasn't about me, it wasn't about my works or about my good deeds. It was about what Jesus did on the cross that made me righteous. Ephesians 2:8-9 says, "For it is by grace [God's remarkable compassion and favor drawing you to Christ] that you have been saved [actually delivered from judgment and given eternal life] through faith. And this [salvation] is not of yourselves [not through your own effort], but it is the [undeserved, gracious] gift of God; not as a result of [your] works [nor your attempts to keep the Law], so that no one will [be able to] boast or take credit in any way [for his salvation]." (Ephesians 2:8-9 AMPC)

After almost two decades of praying and believing, I received a true understanding of God's grace. I finally came to the end of myself, and the Holy Spirit revealed my heart to me. My lack of understanding and jealous attitude almost caused me to miss my blessings. And to think I could have ruined all the Lord had for us! I repented, apologized to Nick and my children, and began receiving the message for myself. Here, I realized that even though I had wrong expectations of my family, God still honored my service. All that time in the church and living for Christ, I didn't know that Jesus loved me for me. I remember being in church as a child, watching people catch the Holy Ghost and have these big outbursts of emotion. I never experienced that and thought, "Why don't I feel that?" Here I am sitting in church on the front row. While Pastor Powe was teaching, for the first time in my life, I saw myself as a little girl in my yellow dress in the back of my childhood home, crying as I watched Jesus go to the cross and Him looking back, just at me. It was the first time I knew Jesus loved me, for me, in all those years. I realized He saved me from all the turmoil of my childhood when I probably would have lost my mind.

I didn't run and holler, but I sat in that seat and wept tears of joy. I knew, without a doubt, that Jesus died for me and loved me! The work was over, and I was free! I now serve God from a position of love because I know He loves me, not out of duty trying to earn His approval and blessings.

Looking back, I see now it was my obedience to God's design for my marriage, and allowing Nick to lead our family, that led me to the truth of God's Word under Pastor Powe at Revealing Truth Ministries. If I had not been obedient to God's design, I would still be broken or divorced and living in the traditions of the LAW I was raised in.

For the first time, Nick and I were truly aligned. I always let him lead our family in natural matters, but now he was leading our family in spiritual things, too. Now we were cooking with gas! God started to really bless us! I began to love my kids where they were, and our relationship blossomed. I love my children unconditionally, just as Jesus loves me, regardless of their actions.

Hopefully, you see now why finding a church is so important. Your church prompts dialogue around the greater you, rather than the mundane things couples discuss daily. It will encourage discussion around the message the Pastor shares. It will bring agreement or disagreement when you hear the Word.

When there's disagreement, you have a more straightforward path to solving conflicts because you have the Holy Spirit, you have church mentors, and you have your pastors.

One of the most significant benefits of the local church is the community, one that gives you outside input through the lens of precious faith. Your community supports your marriage, gives you space to grow, and helps you to develop your individual and collective gifts and talents. A good church is not only a place for encouragement, but also a place for correction. Being a member of a local church allows both of you to submit to God and align your thinking according to God's will.

Attending a local church helps align your thinking with your spouse according to God's will. We must renew our minds and exchange our thoughts for God's thoughts. Romans 12:2 says, "And do not be conformed to this world [any longer with its superficial values and customs], but be transformed and progressively changed [as you mature spiritually] by the renewing of your mind [focusing on godly values and ethical attitudes], so that you may prove [for yourselves] what the will of God is, that which is good and acceptable and perfect [in His plan and purpose for you]." (Romans 12:2 AMPC)

A career is just a means to an end; a vision is a godly purpose you are graced to do together. Everything that we need is in the church. It allows you to grow and develop independently and collectively. Cultivating a shared vision for your marriage and family will lead to a fulfilling and prosperous life.

Chapter 9

Alignment

As you surrender your marriage to God, alignment will come naturally. When you and your husband align your actions and goals, you will see things in your life fall into place.

Nick and I reached a complete alignment point where we could effectively communicate our goals and desires and dedicate ourselves to serving our church and pastors. We purchased two homes and achieved financial stability. We even experienced a miraculous IRS debt cancellation of $265,000 from when Nick mishandled our taxes from NAMS, our business. We were terrified to contact the IRS, and our credit was in shambles. We only used cash for years, and the IRS even began to garnish our wages at one point. It was a complete disaster.

While at Revealing Truth Ministries, Pastor Powe told Nick to repay all of our debts due to the calling on our lives. We needed to be above reproach, so we had to get our lives straight, including our finances. That very same night we attended a financial conference with Pastor Avazni and sowed a seed of $100 for confidence to call the IRS. We certainly weren't expecting the blessing that God had in store for us.

The following day, Nick called, gave all his information, hoping to get a payment arrangement, and the IRS representative told him his debt had been released! What a blessing, right? Nick then proceeds to tell the IRS representative that his pastor told him he HAD to pay it back and asked where he could send the money. The representative told him that he could send it, but that the account was gone so the money would just be returned. We saw the tangible blessing of obeying our man of God; so when Pastor Powe spoke, we obeyed.

I shared this story to show how we have experienced a flow of blessings in our lives. Going from years of struggling, to now watching it all fall into place in a few short years helped keep me in line with our vision. I even turned down a job promotion with a wage increase because it didn't align with our vision.

During my son's elementary school years, I worked as a Paraeducator for special needs children. When I arrived at the school, I was assigned to one particular boy, that was being disregarded and neglected by the staff due to his inability to communicate. The staff was scared he would have a meltdown, so they isolated him in a corner with no interaction and no work. As a result, he became bored and began to eat random things like pencil shavings and paper. So being me, I used humor and playfulness to bring him out of his shell. Whenever he ate something inappropriate, I made silly faces and warned him, "Don't eat that!" Gradually, he became like a miniature version of me.

He started to speak up and became more sociable. If I put my hands in my pockets, he would do the same. The rest of the staff was amazed by his transformation and always asked me how I did it. I prayed for him, and he became a completely different person - friendly, engaging, and intelligent! He had an amazing personality and he was so funny that he would have the entire class in fits of laughter. Eventually, he started participating in class and finishing assignments.

One day I was with another staff member, and she told me, "I don't know what it is, but when you are around, I feel like nothing can go wrong." I experienced what Pastor Powe taught me: the anointing is with me, and it will remove burdens and destroy yokes. The job was sweatless; I was anointed to effect change in their lives. The staff had been previously afraid of the students' meltdowns. Watching adults panic and scramble in response to children's behavior was mind-boggling to me. I would walk up and take command of the situation. I was never mean; I spoke with love and authority, and the kids responded. Eventually, I ended up with the original little boy's two sisters as well, who were also autistic.

When the time came for my job evaluation — honestly, I was nervous; it was the first time I had a professional evaluation. The principal was so pleased with my work and the children's progress under my care that she offered me a permanent position and even offered to pay for a fast-track accreditation! I was so proud of myself.

I felt I had found a place to make a meaningful impact on kids' lives and to advance my education!

I went home to tell Nick and my kids the good news. I knew we were close to being released to start our ministry in Orlando, but we had yet to be sent out. I spoke with Nick about it, and he said it wouldn't work. I was thinking of ways to make it work, but the program was only for the schools in Hillsborough County in Tampa and not for Orange County in Orlando, where we were moving. I reluctantly declined. Although I knew God had better opportunities as I trusted Him, I must admit it was bittersweet to decline the offer. Sure enough, about a month later, Pastor Powe released us to start Life Transforming Ministries, so we packed up and headed to Orlando, which was easily the greatest adventure of my life!

Upon arriving in Orlando, I was excited to see what God had in store for us. Despite Nick having management experience, when we got to Orlando he started work under John, a salesman whom he had previously managed. Meanwhile, I searched tirelessly for employment, but unfortunately, school year had already begun, and I was too late for paraeducator positions. Nick was making a fraction of what he had made and was also looking for a better-paying job.

Nick went to an interview and told them he was a pastor and would have to leave work if his pastor called him. The interviewer started saying ugly things about Billy Graham.

Nick defended Pastor Graham, saying he was one of the greatest men of God on earth. Nick was offended and told the interviewer off and warned him not to say another word about Billy Graham. I called Nick and asked how the interview went; he said, "I don't think I'll be getting that job," and told me what happened. But two hours later, the company called Nick and offered him the job. He told Nick he respected the fact that he was willing to stand up for what he believed. Nick made his first million dollars that year, and I never found or needed a job again!

It's not a coincidence that we were released into ministry once we got to this point in our marriage. When you know your vision, and you and your husband are walking in lockstep, you will see the blessings increase in your life. Your marriage will have a purpose, and the best part is that the things that used to cause major arguments in your marriage won't even matter anymore!

Fight for Your Marriage

Let's discuss your marriage and where you stand. Take a moment to ask yourself, "Where am I in this? Have I given up, or am I still fighting for what I know is mine to have?"

Throughout this book, I have primarily addressed women. You may be wondering why I haven't addressed men as much since they are the heads of the household. That is because God has given women the power to win over their husbands, and women have the power to make or break their marriage. So, I addressed this book to the one who has the power to empower through love: the WOMEN!

I know many of you are one foot in and one foot out; however, I want to encourage you to fight for your marriage! We often think the grass is greener on the other side of the fence, but when we get to the other side, we discover the grass is really weeds. It's all an illusion.

Why should you fight for your marriage? What happens if you don't fight for your marriage and give up? Let's look at the potential outcomes of ending your marriage.

Divorce

Let me be clear: GOD IS NOT FOR DIVORCE, but it is an option if you or your child are being physically abused. God did not call us to bondage. There are other reasons that divorce may be permissible, such as adultery. I know this betrayal can hurt you to your very core. However, we all come short of the glory of God, and anyone is due a second chance. Remember, God forgave you when you missed it. My advice is to seek the Holy Spirit and your pastors. If you don't have pastors, seek Christian marriage counseling about what to do for your situation, and don't move until you get peace about it. Colossians 3:15 AMPC says, "And let the peace (soul harmony which comes) from Christ rule (act as umpire continually) in your hearts [deciding and settling with finality all questions that arise in your minds, in that peaceful state] to which as [members of Christ's] one body you were also called [to live]. And be thankful (appreciative), [giving praise to God always]." (Colossians 3:15 AMPC)

If you decide to divorce, it can bring you and your family even more trauma, drama, and poverty, especially if you have children. Your children will have to split their time between two homes, which can be a source of stress and instability for them, disrupting their sense of home life, especially if you do not approve of the person your ex-husband is now dating or chooses to marry.

As a woman, you will likely be the sole financial provider for your household. This means you will have to take care of your children and manage your home alone. You may have to work extra hours at your job to make up for the loss of income, which could result in less time spent with your children. In other words, you will carry the whole kit and caboodle!

Throughout my book, I've talked about how men and women are equal in the eyes of God. However, men and women are not equal in the realm of dating, particularly as they age. As men grow older, their dating prospects do not change. They don't have to wait to be approached or proposed to. In fact, most men can still attract younger, attractive women who are willing to marry them, not because they love them, but to use them, provided they are financially stable. As women age, their physical attraction changes, which can significantly decrease their dating prospects. The reason I am mentioning this is because there are seasons to life. When women are younger, they are beautiful, innocent, easily influenced, impressed, and it's easier for men to feel like their hero.

So if you leave your husband thinking you will get a young strapping buck that will whisper sweet nothings in your ear, like in your younger days, this is not reality. You may be thinking, "Pastor Frannie, yes, I can get a younger man who will whisper sweet nothings in my ear." My answer to that is you probably can. However, you will be a mom with benefits, better known as a cougar, which is no real relationship or love. You will be used for your experience, sex, and gifts. These boys will more than likely leave you for someone younger when you're older, leaving you high and dry. As men and women grow older, relationship dynamics change and the dating game is not the same because you are in a different season of life.

You may be considering plastic surgery as a way to reverse the effects of aging and compete with younger women. However, it's important to be cautious when it comes to plastic surgery. Some procedures can go wrong, leaving you in debt, in chronic pain, with prolonged hospital stays, and even worse, can result in death. We all get older; it's a part of life! No matter what you do, you are going to age! We must love ourselves and cultivate inner beauty. Inner beauty is what captivates the heart forever!
I truly believe the feminist movement gave women the notion that men are expendable; they are no longer necessary and can be

easily replaced. A woman can do anything that a man does or even better. This type of thinking is straight from the pit of hell; marriage is about teamwork and not competition. It's important to remember that many celebrities who sing or rap about certain lifestyles may actually live differently in real life. For example, they may create songs about being independent and leaving men, to make money but in reality, they are married and even fight to keep their marriages intact. Many who fall prey to this philosophy will end up alone, lonely, and searching for love and companionship later in life, which makes it much more challenging to secure a husband at this stage. We believe in the omnipotence of God and that He can do anything. He is a God who restores, and when we renew our minds, replace our thoughts with His, and fully surrender to Him, He will fulfill the desires of our hearts.

Many single women are waiting and believing in God for a husband. While you may think that finding a new husband will bring fun and excitement into your life, it's important to remember that there are many men out there who are only looking for vulnerable women for casual sex and have no intention of getting married. Starting over is not easy, so if you are already married, it's better to work on rekindling your love with your husband instead of seeking a new relationship.

Every relationship requires hard work, effort, and forgiveness. Make godly decisions and fight for your marriage to have a prosperous, peaceful, happy and true love connection!

Separation

You may consider separation from your husband, don't do it! If your spouse is unwilling to attend counseling and you cannot change his mind, he needs to decide if he wants to remain married or not. You can't have your cake and eat it, too! It takes two willing parties to save a marriage.

When I married Nick, I made one of the best decisions when I told him that if he ever wanted to leave, he could. We would be done for good, though! I told him that if he left, he wouldn't ever darken my doorstep again, that we would correspond by letter or phone concerning our children, and that when he came to pick up the kids, they would be in the driveway waiting for him! Let me tell you, that forewarning worked; we have never separated in forty years. God is not about confusion. An endless cycle of separating and then getting back together is not honoring Him. It will diminish your self-esteem and the respect you should have for yourself as well. 1 Corinthians 14:33 says, "For God is not the author of confusion but of peace, as in all the churches of the saints." (1 Corinthians 14:33 NKJV)

Trial separations and breakups are just a license to go out, sleep around, and produce illegitimate children and bring more trauma to the marriage. How can your spouse truly miss you or know they've left a good thing if you allow them to come back and forth, in and out of your life, whenever they want to? James 1:7-8 says, "For truly, let not such a person imagine that he will receive anything [he asks for] from the Lord, [For being as he is] a man of two minds (hesitating, dubious, irresolute), [he is] unstable and unreliable and uncertain about everything [he thinks, feels, decides]." (James 1:7-8 AMPC)

Whatever you compromise to keep, you have already lost. Don't waste time with someone who won't commit to you wholeheartedly. The dating game really is different for women than men, especially in later seasons of our lives.

The option I highly recommend when times are tough in your marriage is to focus on your relationship with God, submit your marriage and your life as a service to God, and allow Him to bless it according to His Word. People enter marriages for many reasons, and some never acknowledge God. I realize this because I was married for years with a form of godliness but no knowledge of the power or grace of God.

To get the best out of your marriage, you need to construct a solid foundation for it to stand on, and there's no better foundation than the Word of God. We cannot truly fulfill or be fulfilled in marriage or life until we honor God's design.

So, I submit unto you that this is your chance to repair the foundation. This could start with repentance and rededicating your life to Jesus Christ. For some of us, that might be joining God's family, which means obtaining salvation and building a relationship with Him like no other for the first time. God wants to bless your marriage, He wants to bless your life, and He wants a relationship with you. It was that relationship that sustained me and gave me hope during the hard times of my marriage. So, fight for your marriage and build a wonderful life with the one you love!

How to Claim Your Salvation!

One thing I want to make abundantly clear: the principles in this book are for believers. Can you apply the principles and see changes? Sure. However, you must be a born-again Christian to get the complete package. After all, marriage was created by God; it's His system. I want to take the time to extend salvation to you. It's not hard or spooky; it's simply confessing with your mouth and believing in your heart that Jesus is Lord. Once you invite Him into your life, He will be there to lead and guide you!

I want to make sure that you have the opportunity to get saved today.

No matter who you are or what you've done, it's not greater than what Jesus did for you when He died for you. He loves you, and you can start fresh today. So, if you've never been saved or asked Jesus to come into your heart, no worries. If you're ready, we can take care of that right now! We will read just four scriptures and get your place in Heaven secured today and on the path to an abundant life here on earth. Let's start at Romans 3:23 which says,

"Since all have sinned and are falling short of the honor and glory which God bestows and receives." (Romans 3:23 AMPC)
We've all missed it. No one is perfect, which is great because we wouldn't need Jesus if we were perfect.

Next, let's go to Romans 6:23, which says, "For the wages which sin pays is death, but the [bountiful] free gift of God is eternal life through (in union with) Jesus Christ our Lord." (Romans 6:23 AMPC)This salvation we're talking about is a gift. You don't have to work for it. It's here and ready for you.

Now for the good part! Romans 10:9-10 says, "Because if you acknowledge and confess with your lips that Jesus is Lord and in your heart believe (adhere to, trust in, and rely on the truth) that God raised Him from the dead, you will be saved. For with the heart a person believes (adheres to, trusts in, and relies on Christ) and so is justified (declared righteous, acceptable to God), and with the mouth he confesses (declares openly and speaks out freely his faith) and confirms [his] salvation." (Romans 10:9-10 AMPC)

It's just that simple! Confess and believe!

Let's bring it all home to John 10:10 says, "The thief comes only in order to steal and kill and destroy. I came that they may have and enjoy life, and have it in abundance (to the full, till it overflows)." (John 10:10 AMPC)

God has so much in store for you. He wants you to have abundance in every area of your life: health, relationships, money, joy, peace, marriage, everything!

All right, are you ready to make this official? Lift your hands and repeat after me:

Father God, I thank you for your son, Jesus. Thank you for sending Him to die for me. I am a sinner, but today I confess with my mouth that Jesus Christ is Lord. Come into my heart. Live in me, lead me, and guide my footsteps. Satan, I serve notice to you. You no longer have power over me. I belong to Jesus Christ; through Him, I will reign, rule, and dominate the earth! As the Word says, I will enjoy life and have it in abundance, to the full, till it overflows! In Jesus Name, Amen!

That's it. Congratulations and welcome to God's family!

Chapter 10

Celebrated not Tolerated

I can hear you in my spirit, "Whew, Pastor, this is all a lot! Is it even worth it?"

YES!!!

God's way is always right; I know where it can take you! Throughout this book, I've shared many of the struggles, sacrifices, and hardships I've encountered in my forty years of marriage. I want to share my experiences and insights on maintaining a successful marriage, which I have documented in my book. These are tried and tested methods that I have lived through that have proven successful. If you desire a prosperous life, including fulfilling your purpose and having a love connection like no other, I urge you to practice the things in my book. God's way never fails! My life is like a dream now, and I want you to have your dreams manifest, too!

Throughout this book, we've discussed the challenges of marriage. However, I want to show you that marriage can be not only good, but it can be fabulous!

God has blessed Nick and me over the years. Things were challenging sometimes, and the relationship didn't always go forth as I had planned, but God worked it out perfectly. We are truly united in our vision and aligned in every way. There were times when Nick pawned ALL my jewelry to feed his gambling addiction, times when the water got turned off, or our cars got repossessed. Now, he wants me to have the best and makes a considerable effort to make that happen.

About two years ago, my four-carat wedding ring was stolen. I took it off before a medical procedure, and I was so upset. I should have secured it better. When I told Nick, I thought he would be angry at me, but instead, he consoled me and told me he would give me double for my trouble. He took his time to find me a new one, not because he didn't want to replace it, but because he wanted to find a beautiful diamond and a custom setting, so it was perfect for me. He finally found the one! He bought me a stunning diamond in a platinum setting, and I will never forget when I saw it. The ring has more carrots than Bugs Bunny could eat, if you know what I mean! I thought, "Oh my God, what have you done!" Nick presented me with a beautiful and completely mesmerizing ring.

I sometimes think about years earlier when Nick pawned my ring in Las Vegas; how shocked and furious I was! I couldn't believe he pawned my wedding ring on our anniversary!
It really showed me how bad Nick's gambling addiction was. Now I think about how he took his time to search for the perfect diamond to replace my stolen ring; it is mind-boggling. He actually has bought me two gorgeous wedding rings. God has really changed him in amazing ways.

What I love most about Nick is that he plans getaways regularly to have me to himself for uninterrupted quality time. Nick has taken me all over the world VIP style! He won't just pick any old hotel either; he knows what I like and will shoot for the stars every time. Nick wants whatever I want. When we went to Europe, he took three days to show me Austria. The reason I wanted to go there was because of the house from "The Sound of Music", a movie I watched every Christmas with my kids. It was magical for me to just set foot in those places, much less visit, have breakfast, and stay on the property! Honestly, Nick could have gone his entire life and not cared about visiting Austria, but he went and enjoyed himself for no reason other than to make me happy.

I don't say these things to boast about my good fortune, and I know you're all saying, "Now, Pastor, we aren't balling like that!" I'm sharing that to compare it to when we didn't understand our family vision and were spiritually and financially broken. I want you to truly understand that my husband has worked to love, cherish, and celebrate me in ways that are significant to me.
I love that he always listens to me; if I say I like something in passing, he will pop up with it later. He holds my hand when we sleep and teases me as a game so that we end up wrestling and chasing each other. He finds reasons to be playful with me, making little jokes, and we both end up in tears, laughing at ourselves. He always reminds me of how good I look, not just a dry, "You look nice," but he calls me beautiful and does so in front of everyone.

Nick is very romantic. He surprised me with a private sunset dinner on the beach at the Ritz Carlton, and I walked out to servers dressed in black ties, torches lit on the beach, music playing, and a candlelit dinner for just the two of us. When we went to Venice, we traveled from Austria by train, and when we got to the dock there, I found Nick had hired a private guide and a Donzi boat, a luxury boat with wood grain, leather seats and windows with curtains; it is the Bentley of boats! He took me to a private island and entered through what they called the James Bond entrance. It was beautiful! My favorite thing he does is when we go to restaurants and I want to try something that I've never had. He will tell me to order it, and then he will get something he knows I like, just in case, so he can switch with me if I don't like what I ordered.

Throughout the day, I get texts telling me he loves or misses me, or if we are together, he will sneak up behind me and whisper Nick loves Frannie, and I'll whisper back, Frannie loves Nick! He knows I struggle with allergies, and when we go away, he will surprise me with maid service at the house so we can come home to a clean place and relax and watch a movie together. He even had my room redecorated behind my back as a surprise. He took me to a Bruno Mars concert in Vegas, and he told me there was a song that reminded him of me, and when they played it, he turned and serenaded me in front of everyone — the song was "Just the Way You Are." He even surprised me with a Maserati for my birthday!

God has blessed us greatly. Nick, to this day, has held many C-level executive positions despite only having a high school education. He makes money outside of the church so he can not only be the King-Priest God has called him to be, taking money from the world and bringing it into the church, but it also affords him the ability to give me the finer things in life and to be a blessing to our family. God has blessed us with millions of dollars over the years through his job selling technology to Fortune 500 companies.

These are just a few examples of how our relationship has gotten to this amazing place since we each understood our role on the team and God's design and purpose for our lives.

Through this book, I hope you can see that no matter where you are in your marriage, if you submit to God's design and pursue Him, you can and will have a love affair with your husband so amazing you will wonder if you are dreaming! Ephesians 3:20 TPT states, "Never doubt God's mighty power to work in you and accomplish all this. He will achieve infinitely more than your greatest request, your most unbelievable dream, and exceed your wildest imagination! He will outdo them all, for His miraculous power constantly energizes you." (Ephesians 3:20 TPT)

Ladies, go forward with confidence! Move beyond tolerating your marriage to celebrating it every day. You have the power to create a love affair with your husband beyond your wildest dreams.

P.S. Nick, my time and experiences without you are meaningless to me. Nothing matters to me, but you, and every day I'm alive, I'm more aware of this. I loved you the day I met you; I love you today and will love you for the rest of my life. ~Love, Frannie

Bibliography

Forbes, B. (2020, July 23). The Hardest Parts Of Marriage (And How To Overcome Them). TheKnot. https://www.theknot.com/content/reddit-marriage-difficulties

Ferguson, A. (2023, October 19). Why Do Women Cheat? Here Are 7 Reasons. WorriedLovers. https://worriedlovers.com/why-do-women-cheat-pl1/

Keepers, D. (2009). The Samaritan Woman at the Well. Faithward. https://www.faithward.org/the-samaritan-woman-disciple-and-evangelist/

Litner, J. (2021, July 2019). What Is Emotional Invalidation? PsychCentral. https://psychcentral.com/health/reasons-you-and-others-invalidate-your-emotional-experience

Montgomery, T. (2023). 7 Benefits of Submission in Marriage. Kingdom Bloggers. https://bloggersforthekingdom.com/submission-in-marriage/

Psych Central. (2022, October 5). Why Do Women Compete with Each Other? PsychCentral. https://psychcentral.com/relationships/competition-among-women

Rainey, B. (2002). What Should Be the Wife's 'Role' in Marriage? FamilyLife. https://www.familylife.com/articles/topics/marriage/staying-married/wives/what-should-be-the-wifes-role-in-marriage/

Rainey, D. (2002). What Should Be the Husband's 'Role' in Marriage? FamilyLife. https://www.familylife.com/articles/topics/marriage/staying-married/husbands/what-should-be-the-husbands-role-in-marriage/

Roelofsz, S. (2023, June 6). What Do Guys Like In a Girl? 31 Qualities of a Highly Attractive Woman.HerNorm. https://hernorm.com/what-do-guys-like-in-a-girl/

Schwantes, M. (2016, August 12). Want a Successful Marriage? Spouses Should Do These 10 Things For Each Other Often. INC. https://www.inc.com/marcel-schwantes/want-a-successful-marriage-spouses-should-do-these-10-things-for-each-other-ofte.html

Slattery, J. (2014, March 26). The Hidden Power of Submission. TCW. https://www.todayschristianwoman.com/articles/2014/march-week-4/hidden-power-of-submission.html

Surtes, O (2022, June 11). What is the Hero Instinct in a Man? HerNorm. https://hernorm.com/what-is-the-hero-instinct/

www.ingramcontent.com/pod-product-compliance
Lightning Source LLC
Chambersburg PA
CBHW060546100426

42742CB00013B/2465